Becoming a Multicultural Church

Becoming a *Multicultural* Church

LAURENE BETH BOWERS

The Pilgrim Press
Cleveland

In dedication to my mother,
Patricia Ann Bryant Bowers

The Pilgrim Press
700 Prospect Avenue
Cleveland, Ohio 44115
thepilgrimpress.com

© 2006 by Laurene Beth Bowers

Materials in the appendix are taken from *And Everyone Shall Praise: Resources for Multicultural Worship* by R. Mark Liebenow. Used by permission.

Biblical quotations are primarily from the New Revised Standard Version of the Bible, © 1989 by the Division of Christian Education of the National Council of the Churches of Christ in the U.S.A., and are used by permission.

All rights reserved. Published 2006

Printed in the United States of America on acid-free paper

11 10 09 08 07 06   5 4 3 2 1

Library of Congress Cataloging-in-Publication Data

Bowers, Laurene Beth, 1958–
    Becoming a multicultural church / Laurene Beth Bowers.
    p. cm.
    Includes bibliographical references (p.   ).
    ISBN 0-8298-1704-2
    1. Church work with minorities–Massachusetts–Randolph–Case studies.
    2. Multiculturalism–Religious aspects–Christianity–Case studies. 3. First Congregational Church (Randolph, Mass.)–Case studies. I. Title.
BV4468.B69 2006
285.8'7447–dc22   2005034128

ISBN 13: 978-0-8298-1704-1
ISBN 10: 0-8298-1704-2

Contents

Introduction / 7

1. And the Lord Sent Plagues: *Problems Afflicting the Segregated European American Community* / 23

2. Parting the Red Sea: *Leadership Empowerment for the Multicultural Movement* / 43

3. The Burning Bush: *Multicultural Images of God* / 53

4. In the Wilderness: *Dynamics of Resistance* / 63

5. Revelation at Mt. Sinai: *Ten Commandments for the Multicultural Church* / 79

6. Melting the Golden Calf: *The Redistribution of Power* / 95

7. A View of the Promised Land: *Envisioning the Multicultural Church* / 113

Notes / 123

APPENDIX A: Seasons of the Church Year / 125

APPENDIX B: Advent Liturgies / 131

APPENDIX C: Resources for Special Days / 143

APPENDIX D: Liturgical, Cultural, and Historical Dates: *Day by Day* / 155

Bibliography / 189

In the final analysis the weakness of Black Power is its failure to see that the black man needs the white man and the white man needs the black man. However much we may try to romanticize the slogan, there is no separate black path to power and fulfillment that does not intersect white paths and there is no separate white path to power and fulfillment, short of a social disaster, that does not share that power with black aspirations for freedom and human dignity. We are bound together in a single garment of destiny.

—Dr. Martin Luther King, Jr.,
Where Do We Go From Here: Chaos or Community? (1967)

Introduction

A FEW YEARS AGO, a host from *Good Morning America* interviewed Fred Caldwell, pastor of an African American church in Louisiana. In the interview, Caldwell spoke of a vision that he believed God had revealed to him, a vision of the kingdom of God where all God's children live in peace with one another and respect one another's cultural background. This vision inspired the church to implement strategies of evangelism in order to shift its membership toward racial diversity. When after several attempts this goal had not been achieved, church members decided to pay five dollars to every white person willing to worship with them on Sunday morning. Even though paying people to attend worship might extend beyond our comfort zone, Caldwell effectively alerted people to the fact that the time has come to begin the journey to become a multicultural church.

After graduating from Andover Newton Theological School in 1983, I served three churches in the United Church of Christ, where membership was predominantly middle-class European Americans between the ages of fifty and seventy. Each of these churches was representative of New England congregationalism. They were similar in their expectation of a traditional style of worship, one that contained a sermon, hymns sung from the *Pilgrim Hymnal,* and collected an offering. The power of each church was centralized to a group of fifteen long-term members. As the pastor, I was just as comfortable as they were to sustain the status quo (i.e., "the way we have always done things"), and I would not have made any significant changes without the approval of those fifteen people whom I sought to please. It was beyond my realm of thinking that the pastor and church had the option to function any differently.

When it came time to search for a fourth church to serve as pastor, I believed that God was calling me to serve a multicultural church. The problem was that I didn't know what that meant or what a multicultural church looked like. At that time, I equated "multiracial" with "multicultural," and so I searched for a church whose membership was racially diverse. But as I searched in 1997, there was not one racially diverse church in the United Church of Christ seeking a new pastor. I complained to God, "But I thought you wanted me to serve a multiracial church!" I believe that the response was if I couldn't find a racially diverse church, I was called to transform a white, segregated one. This commission overwhelmed me because I was clueless about how to go about doing that. So in typical prophetic fashion, I whined to God that there had to be someone else out there more qualified than I. But once again God called the least likely, only to assure that we witness God's intervention in the world.

I was called to First Congregational Church in Randolph, Massachusetts. The church is located in the center of the most racially diverse town in Massachusetts, just twelve miles south of downtown Boston.[1] It is an urban, almost inner-city environment. Some of the towns closer to Boston tend to attract immigrants because there they can find more affordable housing. But when immigrants assimilate through education and employment, they tend to move out of the inner city and into communities such as Randolph, where there is racial and ethnic diversity. Randolph's ethnic composition is comprised of groups who seek to move away from the economically depressed environment and into more desirable neighborhoods. Those who have shifted their economic status to be able to afford to live in the suburbs are hesitant about moving into all-white neighborhoods. They want to protect their children from being victims of prejudice, and they seek to preserve their own cultural heritage through communal living with those from their own ethnic or racial background. In the town of Randolph, there is a clearly marked racial division between white long-term residents and persons of color whose socioeconomic status is moving upward.

On its conference profile, the church described itself as "a traditional, elderly congregation with an average attendance of 130." The membership was almost exclusively European Americans who had lived in Randolph all of their lives. Like many churches situated in neighborhoods experiencing an influx of ethnic and racial diversity, the membership was not changing to reflect that diversity. The church was operating under the assumption that given time, and if they were friendly to visitors, its membership would consequently become multiracial. But when I interviewed with the search committee, they shared members' growing concern that this would not happen without a plan of action. I realized then that God was calling me to lead them in this endeavor.

Today the church is a multiethnic, multiracial community. Because we don't use those terms any longer, members will tell you that they attend "a multicultural church." Together, we set out as sojourners along a journey that would free us from several problems of the past, move us into the wilderness, and give us vision to see the promised land. This book shares our journey with the reader. We learned that a multicultural church does not just happen but is a result of prayerful strategic planning. God needs instruments to accomplish God's will and purposes. To become a multicultural church, leaders are called to be *faithful* to where God may be leading, *intentional* about discerning God's plan of action, and *persuasive* that others may follow.

This book is titled *Becoming a Multicultural Church* to emphasize our common mission as Christians to be united as the universal church, that is, the body of Christ. If one or two churches manage to become multicultural, they may be "tokens" and enable other churches to maintain their segregated status, i.e., "We're not multicultural, but there are multicultural churches in our conference!" (As a pastor of a multicultural church, I often feel protective of the congregation, for instance, against those who want to come in and take pictures on Sunday morning.) Our call at this point in time is to encourage other churches to become multicultural so that our sisters and brothers in Christ can come with us to the promised land. We perceive the journey to be one of *cooperation* among the churches, rather than *competition* for seekers in the community.

Why I was the One to Write this Book

I might have been considered the least likely person to go to seminary in spite of the fact that I felt called to be a parish minister since the third grade. (When asked the question, "What do you want to be when you grow up?" I replied "a minister.") As a teenager, all my friends teased me, saying "You don't seem like the type." I wrestled with the angel who insists that all ministers fit the standard model. Growing up in the 1960s and early 70s, all the ministers of my church had been white men. One Sunday morning in church, while we were singing a hymn out of the *Pilgrim Hymnal,* I turned to my mother and asked, "Mom, can women be ministers, too?" And my mother, in her wisdom, answered back, "Women can be anything that they want to be." I thank God my daughter doesn't have to ask.

When I was interviewed recently, I made the comment that, because I am a woman, there are still some people in the community who will say, "You don't look like a minister." But when the interview appeared in print, it read, "Rev. Bowers admits that she doesn't look like a minister." The following Sunday, I was blessed by that angel when, as a mouthpiece for God, I said from the pulpit, "If I have been a parish minister for the past twenty-plus years, then I am what a minister looks like!" It has taken me many years to appreciate that God called me to the parish ministry because I don't fit the traditional mold. We tend to assume that God calls persons who are different in spite of their difference, rather than because of it.

I am also the least likely person to write a book on multiculturalism. After I had spoken at a conference on contemporary worship, it dawned on me that what I was really talking about was becoming a multicultural church. (All worship is contemporary.)

So I called the conference office in Massachusetts and asked, "How many other churches in our conference are multicultural or multiracial?" The response was only a few, depending on one's definition of multiculturalism. First Congregational Church of Randolph does not perceive itself as different from any other congregation in the United Church of Christ with one exception: We are becoming multicultural.

A colleague commented to me, "Why are you writing a book on multiculturalism? Shouldn't that book be written by someone who is black?" I write as a middle-class European American heterosexual woman who is theologically conservative and socially liberal. My father is German American, and my mother has Native American ancestry. I grew up with people saying to me, "Your mother looks like an Indian!" and interpreted this as a negative comment. I am the right person to write a book on multiculturalism because I write as a member of the dominant culture to other members of the dominant culture (as if it's a club!), but I do not speak on behalf of all European Americans. And though I write to the dominant European American members of a traditional church, I hope that other ethnic-segregated churches will read the book with interest.

While there are several excellent books on the subject of multiculturalism, they begin with the assumption that the church has already transitioned to become multicultural. There are a few exceptions. I draw the reader's attention to one of the best books on the subject, *The Wolf Shall Dwell with the Lamb* by Eric Law, a Chinese American Episcopalian priest. Interestingly, most of the current literature on multiculturalism is written by persons of color and diverse ethnic backgrounds. Many of the books are written by male pastors or men who refer to male pastors as illustrations of those who are effectively implementing multicultural strategies. I could not find a book by a woman of European American heritage writing to the European American community, and so was inspired to write one.

God has a habit of using the least likely so that there is no question that it is divine intervention. Moses complained that he had a speech impediment (Ex. 4:10) so that the Israelites would know that it was the voice of God speaking through Moses. Jeremiah whined that he was too young to speak on behalf of God to the people (Jer. 1:6.7). Jonah jumped ship, literally, and needed some meditation time in the belly of a fish (Jonah 1:12ff) before he felt qualified to be a prophet. Gideon was instructed to take three hundred men who lapped like dogs to battle (Judges 7:7) so that the Israelites witnessed to the Lord's plan for them. As one of those least likely persons, I have become the right person to speak to others who perceive that they too are among the least likely.

Defining Multiculturalism

In 1993, the General Synod of the United Church of Christ adopted a pronouncement calling the United Church of Christ to be a multiracial and multicultural church. But we need to tweak out the differences between these two terms. Much of the literature on multiculturalism is moving away from using the category of race because those who are African American do not share the same cultural identity as those who are Haitian American.[2] Race, then, is not necessarily an indicator of cultural grouping. I will therefore use this category sparingly. More commonly, we refer to ourselves as a "multiethnic" congregation in terms of cultural composition.

The definition of multiculturalism descended upon the church through the work of the Holy Spirit. When we began talking about becoming multiracial and wondering how to attract persons of color, we witnessed to the surprising grace that we were also attracting persons from the hearing-impaired community. The stronger our efforts to gather persons from different ethnic backgrounds, the more we attracted persons from other marginalized cultural groupings that, historically, had experienced exclusion from the Christian church. We had recently installed an elevator to make our church accessible to those with disabilities but we had not anticipated that persons with physical challenges would then be able to join us for worship. (We thought the elevator was for the elderly.) There was never a time when the church held a congregation meeting to vote on a definition of multiculturalism. Instead, it was chosen for us and seeks to be inclusive of all cultural groupings.

> A multicultural church honors gender, race, ethnicity, sexual orientation, economic situation, age and ability.

According to the *Dictionary of Cultural Literacy,* culture is "the sum attitudes, customs, and beliefs that distinguishes one group of people from another. Culture is transmitted through language, material objects, ritual, institutions, and art from one generation to the next."[3] Culture is learned through a series of interactions with one's grouping and thus a process of socialization (versus biologically induced). It determines the norm of what constitutes socially appropriate patterns of relating. Michael V. Angrosino writes, "Culture is shared in the context of organized social groupings, which are not unitary entities, but networks of relationships based on such factors as race, ethnicity, gender, socioeconomic class, age, condition of 'disability' and sexual orientation."[4] Disability is defined as "the disadvantage of activity caused by contemporary social organization which takes no or little account of people who have physical impairments and thus excludes them from participation in mainstream activities."[5]

The Nature of Prejudice

Becoming a multicultural church requires not only evangelizing persons from diverse cultural groupings but making internal changes as well. If a faith community excludes one of the above cultural groupings, then it will sabotage its efforts to become multicultural. For example, when a church resists calling a female pastor but is interested in increasing its racial diversity, it is still practicing prejudice and will struggle to attract one cultural grouping while excluding another. The problem with prejudice is that it is "free-floating." People who are prejudiced are usually unaware of it, or they perceive that they can conceal it from others. But those who have a history of being excluded or prejudiced against become sophisticated in picking up cues that another person is prejudiced against them or others.

Similarly, when a marginalized person hears the pastor excluding the "other," especially from the pulpit, even if the "other" is not in his or her cultural grouping, that person might fear that his or her cultural grouping will be the target of prejudice in the near future.

If I am an Hispanic American, I might be relieved that prejudice is directed against gays and lesbians because that takes the focus away from my cultural grouping. But I might also be offended that any prejudice is being promoted because I know what it feels like to experience prejudice.

Historically, cultural groupings that are marginalized have had to fight among each other for the crumbs of power falling from the table of the dominant group. These marginalized groups compete with each other for power because to challenge the power of the dominant group seems insurmountable. This dynamic is operative when those in the African American community oppose the civil rights of the gay-lesbian-bisexual-transgendered (GLBT) community. They say, "What about us? Look at the violence that has afflicted our people!" The dominant group has set up a situation in which the marginalized groups have to compete among each other for "the most oppressed" status with the hope of attaining liberation for their own cultural grouping.

To counter resist against this dynamic, a multicultural church builds solidarity among the marginalized groups and confronts the power structure of the dominant group. It brings together persons of historically marginalized groups to build strength in their togetherness. But the marginalized group should not be the one who confronts the dominant share nor persuades out of this newly acquired strength. The multicultural church empowers leaders to be skilled in confrontation.

But the dominant group needs to be convinced that it is in their best interests to share their power with the marginalized. It is not our intention to take power away from the dominant group because if they sense that this is happening to them, they are likely to strengthen their resistance. Such an outcome would be counterproductive to achieving our goal. The idea is not to take power away from one group and give it to another—for instance, to make the marginalized group into the dominant group and the dominant group into the marginalized group. Rather, the goal of a multicultural church is to offer a different model of power whereby it is distributed more evenly. I will suggest that the criteria for distribution of power should be based on role and performance.

The present model of power that is used in European American segregated churches is what I refer to as "centralized power." Fifteen people run the church. Pastors tend to enable this status quo when they select a group of friends to form an inner circle. Because pastors radiate power, these parishioners share in the pastor's power in exchange for supporting the pastor (and they only defend the pastor for as long as they perceive that the pastor has power). This creates a network of active parishioners with power versus peripheral parishioners with less power. These dynamics mirror the political structures in our other social institutions. The multicultural church models a new way of sharing power that promotes peace and justice and benefits everyone.

Can Our Church Become Multicultural?

Whenever I speak on the subject of multiculturalism, someone inevitably laments, "But our church is not located in a racially diverse neighborhood!" That depends on one's definition of "neighborhood." It used to be thought that a neighborhood was established by those whom one knows personally. A geographic circle could be drawn around a neighborhood. But the world is changing. People have greater opportunity to interact with persons from across the world. The Internet allows us to converse with persons in faraway lands. Neighborhood now embodies a global village. The question is: Should the Christian church wait for our neighborhoods to become racially diverse, or should it be a forerunner in teaching people how to peacefully relate to each other so that they can live side by side?

It is not unusual anymore for people to commute an hour or more to work five days a week. If participating in a multicultural church is important to them, we should expect that they will also be willing to commute to church. By broadening our concept of the local neighborhood church, we welcome persons from other ethnic groupings who might reside in another community. On Sunday morning, it is expected that many people will drive some distance to attend our church. These people will testify that it is well worth it in order to attend worship in a multicultural church. The goal of multiculturalism is that, as congregations become more racially and ethnically diverse, they will transfer what they have learned in church into the community. The Christian church has the opportunity to be a leader in the multicultural movement by teaching diverse people how to live together. The premise of this book is that *every church can become multicultural*.

Why Would a Church Not Want to Become Multicultural?

There are several reasons why multiculturalism will not work for some churches at the present time. Ethnic-segregated churches that conduct the worship service in their ethnic-specific language provide for those who have yet to learn the English language. These communities also often create a sanctuary from the power of the dominant group, and an opportunity for those who feel powerless in relation to the dominant group, to assert some power within the marginalized group. Ethnic congregations function to preserve cultural traditions held by their parents to be sacrosanct. European American congregations, however, do not gather as segregated communities because of language, preservation of ethnic background, or to assert power that is not available to them elsewhere.

I think there will always be a need for ethnic-segregated congregations, but which ethnic groupings this will include may be transitional over time. For instance, the Haitian American community has for many years been drawn to worshiping in a Haitian-segregated church. But the young generation of Haitian Americans not only knows English but has attended multiethnic schools and are used to relating to the diverse cultures. It is our experience that they are less interested in worshiping in an ethnic-specific congregation but still have a desire to preserve their cultural traditions.

We have responded to this need in two ways: (1) We invite persons to share their cultural traditions in worship. If it is really important to the Hispanic American community that the prayer is prayed in Spanish, then we pray in Spanish. If the African American community is looking for gospel music in worship, then we ask someone to lead gospel music (although everyone can participate). (2) We formed communities within communities to identity and meet the cultural needs that are met in an ethnic-segregated faith community. The purpose is not to disrespect an individual's relationship with his or her ethnic background, but to honor, incorporate, and celebrate it within the larger church.

Why Would a European American Church Want to Become Multicultural?

I became a leader in the multicultural movement because I believe this is the direction that God is leading the Christian church and that God is calling me to be one of those leaders. I also had a selfish reason for wanting to be in a multicultural setting: As the mother of three children, I wanted my children to be raised in a community that would help them become ethnic sensitive and culturally aware. These skills are essential for learning how to conduct business, trade, and commerce on the international level. Children raised in segregated communities will be at a disadvantage because they will have little opportunity to develop these relational skills. As computer technology increases our interaction with persons from other cultural groupings, our ethnic sensitive skills will need to improve as well. The way to help our children to be economically successful is to raise them in a multicultural environment.

Unfortunately, middle-class white persons often perceive racially and ethnically diverse neighborhoods as ridden with drugs and violence. News reporting promotes these perceptions, creating the illusion that nothing good is happening in these communities and people aren't safe. Even movies portray inner-city neighborhoods as a likely setting for car chases, rape, and murder. Sociologically speaking, there is some truth to these perceptions because economics often produces situations where people have no other option than to risk illegal activity. But the consequence is that European Americans link violence with racial and ethnic diversity. Given these misperceptions, why would any church intentionally work toward becoming culturally diverse?

In the midst of writing this book, my son Kyle and two of his friends were robbed at knifepoint. One of his friends was stabbed. Those who attacked them took their wallets and cell phones, and because I was in Chicago at the time and my son's car wasn't working, they took my keys to the car, the church, etc. When Kyle called me, he said, "Three black kids robbed us." I responded, "They were three kids who were also black." He knew what I meant. I continued, "They robbed you of your stuff, but please don't let them rob you that you were raised to resist the forces of prejudice." Undoubtedly, some will ask, if those in the marginalized group have historically been victimized and are angry, why would we want those people in our church on Sunday morning? (We also have to ask, why would they want to come?) The multicultural church respects the history of tension, conflict, and violence that has occurred between the races.

We also have to ask: Why is segregation a problem today? Historically, as we well know, almost all social institutions were segregated. Along came affirmation action and equal-employment opportunities, and these same social institutions became racially and ethnically integrated. The days of signs that professed exclusion, i.e., "whites only," are now illegal. And yet there are more subtle ways that we send signals of exclusion. People do not need a sign to know where they are not welcome. Even though it is evident that prejudice still infiltrates these systems in both overt and subtle manifestations, e.g. not everyone receives the promotion they deserve, most social organizations are becoming multicultural.

Many people have also had the opportunity to learn new patterns of relating to culturally diverse persons in settings other than the church. For instance, those who attend college are more likely today to interact with culturally diverse persons. When they attend a segregated white church, it appears to them to be an outdated relic of the past. Why has the Christian church not been like other social institutions in changing its membership? It makes young people wonder whether a church that remains segregated must want to be so. When one of our young people recently attended another church, he came back with the observation, "Everyone there was white!"

One other issue was to determine which church would become multicultural. Initially people said, "If they want to be part of our church, let them come here." No one said, "Let's close our doors and move down the street and integrate with a church whose racial composition is different from ours!" People were willing to embark on the journey as long as they never had to leave the pew (or I should say "my pew," as in good ol' congregationalism). As the European American church represents the interests of the dominant group, this became an issue for other cultural groupings. The dominant white group was willing to play with the marginalized groupings as long as they were willing to come to our house.

Why Would Marginalized Person Want to Attend a Segregated Church?

Marginalized people fear that attending a dominant church will not be a liberation in shared power but will mirror their experience of being marginalized in society. In other words, when they attend a church where a dominant group is clearly in power, their experience of marginality is reinforced. The marginalized person has good reason to be suspicious of a European American church that wakes up one day and decides it wants to be something different.

As a marginalized person, if I heard that the congregational church down the street was attempting to reach out to the community so that it could become more racially and ethnically diverse, I might be asking, "Why?" and "Why now?" I would want to know the motivation for this change of heart and what they expect from me. How is my presence in their midst going to change things for them? Because so many churches have been struggling with membership and financial resources, I might be suspect that the only reason they want to attract new members is to help with their financial situation, i.e., "the church only wants my money."

If one church begins the journey toward multiculturalism for reasons that are not theological and/or that neglect to articulate this theological vision, then it could sabotage the efforts of other churches who are along this journey. If a church perceives that reaching out to the community and bringing in new members will resolve its financial woes, then that should be stated clearly (although I would advise against adopting this as the reason). If persons from marginalized cultural groupings attend one church and perceive that its reasons for becoming multicultural are other than theological, they may be less likely to visit another church that is trying to become multicultural for the right reasons.

Levels of Inclusion

I am frequently asked if our church is "open and affirming." In the United Church of Christ, it is a phrase to refer to a level of inclusion with respect to gays and lesbians. There is a formal process of becoming an open and affirming church beginning with conversations in small groups and leading to a congregational meeting when a vote is taken. At First Congregational Church of Randolph, the issue is not whether we should be welcoming of gays and lesbians, but what the phrase "open and affirming" means and the message it conveys.

If I am "open and affirming" of another person or cultural grouping, then I sit on the throne of judgment to decide who gets to come to my church and who does not. That seat comes with tremendous power in that "the way I see it" (focalization) is not only the right way but determines the level of inclusion. When my focalization is the only one that counts, then I am discounting the view of others. A multicultural church teaches people to look through the eyes of others and get a different view of the situation.

There are three levels of inclusion. The first is tolerance. If I am a member of a church that is making the shift from segregation to multiculturalism, but I am not in favor of these changes, I might think that going along with them and keeping quiet is the best approach. I will tolerate a person of a different cultural grouping sitting next to me in the pew because I don't want to be viewed as a person of prejudice, or worse, accused of not being a good Christian. I will keep my prejudices to myself, and no one will ever know. The problem with this way of thinking is that persons who have experienced being marginalized cannot afford to be brought into a community where people of the dominant group only tolerate them. ("I don't need to be around more people who want to keep me in my place.") Also, they are sophisticated in picking up cues of prejudice. ("He was not only prejudiced against me, but he thought I was stupid enough not to be able to tell.")

The second level is to affirm, as in "open and affirming." To this extent, I have some curiosity toward the "other" and want to get to know some of their cultural traditions, but this is so that I can judge whether they fit with my focalization. If I am a heterosexual person, then I get to decide who is "straight" and who is "crooked." The dominant group thus decides the range of normalcy.

The third level is to honor. The word "honor" is used in our definition of multiculturalism because most cultural groupings in the world function as a shame/honor society. What makes honor a step above tolerance and affirming is that it refrains from passing judgment about whether I perceive that the cultural grouping should be included in a social setting. I do not seek to understand it because I do not need to in order to honor someone as a person and respect that person's cultural grouping. This third level respects the worth and dignity of every individual independently of, as well as in affiliation with, his or her cultural grouping. (Individuals are more than the sum of their cultural groupings.)

The Aim of the Book

The purpose of this book is to be inspirational and persuasive. The task that lies before me is to convince the reader that the benefits of becoming a multicultural church outweigh the sacrifices, struggles, and moments of desperation. I intend to equip the reader with strategies to become a leader in the multicultural movement, whether as a lay or ordained minister. I will advise that one of the leaders must be the pastor because without his or her leadership, it will not appear to be an important part of the church's spiritual development. This is a process that demands commitment. The objective is to encourage every member of the faith community to participate. The only way to reach the promised land is together. I have made every effort to write in a conversational style so that the book sounds like a dialogue between friends.

The book is divided into seven chapters. I have subtitled it "a biblical model." I believe that the Israelites' experience of journeying from oppression to liberation and into the promised land is an analogous model for depicting the experience of journeying from segregation to multiculturalism. We begin by identifying the plagues or problems afflicting the European American church.

Leaders of the multicultural movement will part the Red Sea waters and lead us into the wilderness, where our spirituality will be broadened as we discover multicultural images of God. No doubt, some will want to regress and return to the way we've always done things. Once in the wilderness, we will prepare for the promised land by receiving rules for interacting with persons of diverse cultural groupings. We will also identify a new model for the church so that power will be more evenly channeled. Finally, we will stand on top of the mountain of God and view the promised land.

I invite you to join me for the journey.

Chapter One

And the Lord Sent Plagues

Problems Afflicting the Segregated Anglo-Church

Then the Lord said to Moses, "See, I have made you like God to Pharaoh, and your brother Aaron shall be your prophet. You shall speak all that I command you, and your brother Aaron shall tell Pharaoh to let the Israelites go out of his land. But I will harden Pharaoh's heart, and I will multiply my signs and wonders in the land of Egypt. When Pharaoh does not listen to you, I will lay my hand upon Egypt and bring my people the Israelites, company by company, out of the land of Egypt by great acts of judgment. The Egyptians shall know that I am the Lord, when I stretch out my hand against Egypt and bring the Israelites out from among them. Moses and Aaron did so; they did just as the Lord commanded them." (Ex. 7:1–6)[1]

WHEN WE FIRST BEGAN TALKING with the church about becoming multicultural, not everyone shared our enthusiasm. Some people insisted, "It will happen if we let it." Since our church appears full each Sunday, some wondered "why would we want any more people?" Others concluded, "If its not broken, don't fix it." As time progressed, however, it became clear that we were experiencing problems that afflicted our level of comfort as a segregated church. Through a process of discernment, it dawned on us that God was sending signs to get our attention. First, we needed to convince the dominant group why marginalized groups should be included. Second, we needed to convince the marginalized groups to come to our church.

I will refer to three distinct groups when talking about the "dominant group." First is the entire European American population. In America, European Americans have been in the majority since Native Americans were displaced to reservations. They continue to hold the most power through political, social, and religious structures. Second is the Christian church. Historically, Christianity has dominated other religions. A prime example was the closing of stores on Sunday to observe the Christian Sabbath. Third is the "dominant group" within the local church. While the focus in this book is convincing the dominant group in the church to share its power, it is important to note that our society has a long history of tolerating injustices that sustain the unequal distribution of power.

Marginalized groups are those who have experienced exclusion, control, oppression, or manipulation by the dominant group. Most people have had the experience of being part of both groups, depending on circumstances or social location. For instance, as a European American, I am part of the dominant group, but as a woman in a traditionally male profession, I also know what it is like to be in the marginalized group.

The Israelites are depicted as the marginalized group in the biblical narrative of the exodus from Egypt. God commissioned Moses to speak to Pharaoh imploring him to let the people go. "But Moses spoke to the Lord, 'The Israelites have not listened to me; how then shall Pharaoh listen to me, poor speaker that I am?'" (Ex. 6:12). The marginalized group has good reason to be suspicious of the traditional European American church that begins the process toward multiculturalism. They might ask, "Why do they want me to join them?" Moses recognized that the marginalized group was not listening to him. Perhaps he assumed that they were not listening because he was unable to communicate in such a way that would persuade them to follow him across the Red Sea.

Pharaoh, who represents the interests of the Egyptians, has an investment in the status quo, i.e., sustaining "the way that it had always been done," because he benefits by keeping the Israelites enslaved. The task before Moses is to convince the dominant group to let go of its power and share it with the marginalized group so that they can go into the wilderness and worship God.

Similarly, the dominant group in a church, which seemingly represents the interests of the entire congregation, perceives that everyone benefits because they run the church. This misperception creates and sustains an unequal distribution of power: Some people in the church have power to make decisions while others have less power or are powerless. The latter groupings represent the powerless group *within* the church. The dominant group might worry that if they shared their power with the powerless, the powerless would seek more power and therefore would try to steal power from the dominant group. The dominant group, which actually hoards the power, fears that if they acquiesce and involve others, the powerless will in turn, hoard power from them. The more afraid the dominant group is of losing power, the more they hoard it. While it might appear that the dominant group is comfortable, they have to worry about someone taking away their power. Nothing short of divine intervention would force them to voluntarily relinquish power.

One way the dominant group works to keep its power from the marginalized group is to keep marginalized cultural groupings from coming to the church in the first place. One Sunday morning an African American family from the South visited our church. The father approached an usher and asked, "Are we allowed to attend this church?" The usher knew that even today in some churches, African Americans are not welcome. After the usher assured him they were welcome, the family came in and sat down in a pew. This experience made our church more aware that people still perceive they are excluded because of their cultural grouping. Those who have been victims of exclusion represent the marginalized group *outside* of the church. Some dominant groups are invested in keeping marginalized groups out of the church. Outside, they are not a threat to their power.

So the Lord sent a series of plagues to afflict the comfortable. Afterward, Pharaoh couldn't wait to get rid of the Israelites (Ex. 12:31). Individuals and social systems are most willing to change their behavior when they find themselves in a situation that causes pain, struggle, and frustration. Individuals who realize that a certain pattern of relating is no longer working might seek a therapist who will enable them to learn effective social skills. These new skills may bring greater satisfaction in their relationships. Similarly, when social systems experience a crisis, they have two options: (1) sustain their current pattern of functioning to the point of nonexistence (i.e., social-system suicide); or (2) make an intentional decision to do things differently. Oftentimes, organizations would rather die than change.

The social system of the Christian Church is presently in a crisis situation. It has the option to continue the model of power that is unequally distributed between the dominant group and the marginalized group. This model, however, seems to promote the loss of members and produce financial struggles. Operating in this mode does not seem to promote a healthy church. In fact, many mainline churches are dying. Fortunately, there is another option. The church can change the way it functions. I suggest a threefold process. First, the church must admit its problems. As prescribed in Alcoholics Anonymous, the first step to recovery is to admit that there is a problem. Second, the church must envision how to do things differently and have the faith to function under these new set of guidelines. Third, the church must be committed to change in such a way that when it is enacted, everyone in the church benefits, and the church is in a better state than when it started the process.

Law advises multicultural leaders to shift their attention away from the dominant group that tends to expect leaders to pay attention to them because they have power.[2] Members of the dominant group are the ones who voice their concerns, complaints, and criticisms to the pastor. In many cases, the pastor tends to pay attention to the ones who yell the loudest. In this chapter, however, I will focus my attention on the dominant group because it is the target group for change. It would be unjust to bring the marginalized group into the church if the dominant group did not want it there. Nothing would be worse for the Christian church to say to members of the marginalized group, "Please come, we want you to join us," and then exclude them from everything. Exclusions can include not meeting their spiritual needs in worship; not being welcoming at fellowship events; not asking them to serve on committees and positions of leadership. It is as if the dominant group is saying, "You can come in . . . but only so far."

I believe that God has sent a series of plagues to convince the dominant group that hoarding power is not working for them or for anyone else. We need to challenge their focus. They need to learn that the way they see it is not the way that everyone sees it. We need to confront their ethnocentric perspective that says the church should function their way. Their way is not the only way, nor is it necessarily the right way. The first questions that need to be asked are: How do we get the dominant group to admit that there is a problem? How can they be moved to envision a different way of functioning at a higher level, whereby everyone is happier and closer to Christ?

From Whence Do We Begin?

It is rather ironic that the Christian church was a forerunner in the abolitionist and civil rights movements, yet remains one of the most segregated institutions in contemporary society. In 1957, Liston Pope observed that "eleven o'clock on Sunday morning is the most segregated hour of the week."[3] Almost fifty years later, European Americans continue to worship in white churches and African Americans worship in black churches. Those who seek to justify segregation in order to sustain it comment, "People want to worship with their own kind," and "We live in a white neighborhood. What are we suppose to do, bus black people in?" The surest way to legitimize segregation is to concede "that the church has always been like this."

The church's advocacy for racial justice alongside its maintenance of segregation, pronounces an ambiguous message to the community at large. Steven Rhodes writes,

> In the civil rights struggle, the church in essence has said to our culture, "Do as we say not as we do." We said to culture that it was a moral imperative to integrate our schools, workplaces and neighborhoods

while simultaneously preserving the segregation that we practice in our services of worship. By refusing to embody the truth claims of the gospel we preached to our culture we lost our credibility.[4]

Whereas the church sought to motivate the community to practice racial and ethnic justice, it contradicted its own mandate. In essence, the church has shot itself in the foot.

What is a segregated church? It is a church whose membership is homogeneous. This means that the membership is predominantly comprised of one ethnic or racial grouping. (European American is considered one ethnic grouping, but it is really a combination of ethnic groupings.) Segregated churches often evangelize an ethnic grouping to preserve their cultural traditions, e.g,. language. The mission of these churches is to preserve cultural identity. In contrast, traditional European American churches have a different reason for being. They function to sustain the power of the dominant group. The white painted church that sets on the hill in the center of town with a steeple reaching to the heavens–the church filled with white people on Sunday morning–appears as a symbol of power, especially in a racially or ethnically diverse neighborhood.

The church that does not reach out to the community has an implicit statement of evangelism: We don't particularly care one way or another if you come. To do nothing communicates to the community that they are not welcome. Most churches' evangelism statement is: "Come if you want. If not, we understand." But this exclusion is often more overt. A church that does not have an elevator to the sanctuary does not want disabled persons to join them for worship. A church that does not have a place to change a baby is not looking to attract young families. A church that does not advertise in the paper, go door-to-door, pass out brochures, invite friends and family, etc., is maintaining its dominion in the midst of the community. Outside and within, people look for indicators to determine whether a church will welcome them and is genuinely looking for other people to join them on Sunday morning.

The second characteristic of the European American segregated congregation is that the power is centralized, typically among fifteen long-term members. The pastor often perceives that he or she needs to consult with these people before making a major decision. It is seemingly irrelevant whether those in the dominant group currently serve on committees or in leadership positions. They retain their power no matter what current position they hold, based on their long association with the church and their investment in getting others to perceive them as "good church members." They also overestimate their level of importance in the life of the church, i.e., "What would this church do without me?" They are often asked to serve on multiple committees in order to spread their power over as a wide an area as possible. Their aim is to make sure the new people are aware of their elevated status. In response to a decision being made that they disagree with, or when they perceive that they might be losing power or fear that another group is emerging to challenge their power, they will often say, "But this is my church!"

Members of the dominant group have convinced themselves that if they let go of their power and share it with others, "The church will close, and we'll end up having to join with another church down the street." They cling to irrational thoughts, made rational in their minds, in order to justify hoarding their power. Because they may feel powerless in other relationships in their lives, which is often the psychological reason that people hoard power in churches, their self-esteem rests upon their ability to sustain that power. Their perception is that their whole world depends on that power. It does not occur to them that shifting power to the marginalized group might actually free them to experience a higher level of personal functioning. They perceive that others respect them because they have power. It is a surprising grace when they realize that other parishioners will still love them, even if they share their power with others.

Plague #1: *Decline in Attendance and Membership*

I grew up in a United Church of Christ (UCC) congregation in suburban Boston during the 1960s and 1970s. My family was active in the church: My mother was the organist and my father served on committees. We attended this church every Sunday morning, and I remember walking two miles in the midst of a snowstorm because we weren't going to miss church. When I was a teenager, I participated in the junior high youth fellowship, which attracted at least twenty-five kids on a regular basis. I recently spoke with a member of this church who shared her frustration that today there are twenty-five people in Sunday morning worship attendance. Where have all the people gone?

Why did the mainline Protestant church flourish up until the 1980s? The Protestant churches all seem to have the same story. They remember the glory days of the 1950s through 1970s, when churches needed to build educational wings to accommodate all the new children that were attending their church. During the Vietnam War there were few people who did not attend a faith community, and churches responded to a societal need by examining the issues pertinent to a national struggle, i.e., whether we should be at war. The community turned to the church not for the answers, but to help them discern the right questions. The church rose to the challenge and was viewed as an influential institution.

One day I decided to go around and ask people whom I did not know in our neighborhood about their perception of the church. Most imagined that on Sunday morning "there are thirty little old ladies singing 'Rock of Ages.'" When I asked if they were interested in attending church, they said, "No, because the church is out of touch with what's going on." The perspective from the outside looking in is that the church has disconnected itself from contemporary issues for fear of being seen as controversial. This was especially true for those who thought we were still a white church in a racially diverse community. Thus, a major barrier to evangelizing and alleviating the plague of declining church attendance and membership is the perception that the church is an outdated institution. The problem is that there is some truth to this perception: The church is functioning the same way it did fifty years ago.

In the 1960s and 70s, the church was willing to try new things; it had nothing to lose because stewardship was producing huge endowments and the pews were filled with people every week. The church was positively reinforced for its functioning. Like giving candy to a child for good behavior, the church continued to do things the same way for the next fifty years, expecting the same results. Meanwhile, society was changing and the church continued "to do things the way we have always done them" even if those things were no longer working. People lament to me in committee meetings, "Ham and bean suppers used to bring in the whole neighborhood, and now no one comes!"

Attracting the young generation has been one of the most challenging contemporary struggles facing the Christian church. Going to church is not an in thing to do. Generation X and Millennials approach religious beliefs differently than a generation ago. With technological and scientific advancements, academia trains the postmodern mind to think critically, logically, and requires proof for the existence of God. In addition, what once was considered sacred time is now time to shop. Children's sports are scheduled on Sunday mornings. Our society has a new phenomenon: a generation of parents who themselves were not brought up in a faith community. These factors contribute to the decline in church attendance.

But perhaps most relevant to our study is that the young generation is used to interacting in multicultural environments. As a result of affirmative action policies and equal employment opportunities, the young generation relates with persons from diverse cultures on a daily basis. Many Generation Xers and Millennials have discovered the benefits of being in a multicultural environment. So when they enter a segregated European American community, something feels weird.

The plague of declining church membership and attendance signals that we should not only change our inward functioning but our outward appearance. The external perception is that the church is out of date, a perception that is reinforced by its lack of cultural diversity. In order to alleviate this plague, the Christian church will need to address contemporary issues. One of the most talked-about issues of our time is multiculturalism and the inclusion of cultural groupings.

Plague # 2: *Spiritual Boredom*

Early on in my ministry, a group of people expressed concern that the teenagers of the church seemed bored with the traditional worship service. As I listened to these concerns, I wondered if the adults were projecting their spiritual boredom onto the teenagers. When something that is going on within ourselves is too uncomfortable for us to admit to ourselves, we think we see it in other people. Teenagers are likely targets for projection because they often look bored in worship. The adults might not have felt comfortable admitting their spiritual boredom for fear of offending the new pastor or being accused of not being a good Christian.

In my previous churches, I had heard these concerns before. Parishioners were bored with worship but as the worship leader, I was unsure about how to remedy this situation. I tried new things in worship, which were initially met with some enthusiasm, but because they didn't address the deeper problem, that enthusiasm was short-lived. So when the issue of spiritual boredom arose in the new church, it was a familiar lament.

I asked, "Why do we want teenagers in worship?" I didn't mean the question to sound sarcastic or disrespectful. I was only curious as to why we would want to do something differently. If the segregated church is experiencing spiritual boredom, the cure might be an unconscious motivation to invite the other to worship. If teenagers are bored with worship, why would anyone expect that having more of them would alleviate the spiritual boredom of the adults? This issue arose further along in the journey when European Americans admitted that they perceived that inviting people of color to worship would make it more lively. After all, "that's the way black people like to worship." In actuality, some black people are attracted to European American churches because they perceived the church to be middle class. They objected to any kind of pastor-parish interaction, because their perception was that it was a style of worship prevalent in "poor black churches.")

Before we decided to speak to the teenagers, we asked ourselves, "Are we willing to change the way we worship?" It would be unfair to ask the teenagers how we might attract them to attend worship if we were not willing to change the way we worship to meet their spiritual needs. We formed a task force to speak with the teenagers. Task force members did so with an open heart and a receptive ear. They conveyed a sense that they genuinely wanted to know how the teenagers felt, and the teenagers expressed to them that they did indeed feel bored. The common denominator that all the teenagers voiced was, "It's not our kind of music."

The task force decided that the teenagers should be invited to play their music during worship. We set certain guidelines, i.e., no swearing, violent, or sexual language. While the songs did not have to be religious, they should convey a message of social justice. Interestingly, the teenagers were actually more worried about the appropriateness of their selections than the adults. Sometimes they even brought a CD to my office to let me hear it and give my approval. They expressed fears of offending the elder generation (whom, incidentally, liked the music almost as much as the teenagers). On one occasion, the wrong song was selected on our CD sound system, and this song contained swears that were now bouncing off every wall in the sanctuary. I anticipated that there would be a line of angry people during coffee hour to speak to the pastor and express their disapproval. But the surprising grace was that everyone guessed what must have happened, and we all laughed.

As we came to respect the spiritual needs of other cultural groupings, we became more aware than ever that worship is not a performance by a worship leader whose job is to entertain the audience. When people complain that worship is boring, I will say, "You're right. If I am supposed to entertain you, I am doing it all wrong." Spiritual boredom is not a result of worship leaders failing to be entertaining. It will not be relieved by finding some new contemporary style of worship by which to "wow" the congregation. It is a plague meant to signal to us that we are uncomfortable in our present way of worshiping. We learned that the problem does not lie with the worship leaders or with the style of worship.

If worship is a performance for a passive audience that judges whether they enjoyed the show, then it would matter little who was in the audience. But worship is a community of persons in relationship. They are the body of Christ, who in some communities refer to themselves as a church family. They pray for one another, share one's another joys and sorrows, and comfort one another in moments of agony and distress. They point to the intervention of God in the past as assurance that God will intervene once again. And if it is not an audience but a congregation of believers, then it does matter who is included in that group.

The most important thing we learned about multicultural worship is this: Worship is a series of interactions between both worship leaders and worshipers as well as worshipers and worshipers. Thus, it matters who is present in the worship service and the extent of cultural diversity among the worshipers themselves.

This means that worship is not geared toward meeting my spiritual needs 100 percent of the time. The only way that might ever happen is in a church with European American middle-class women in their forties who like Pink Floyd and see the world exactly like me (and still we might all disagree). If the entire congregation is just like me, then I have a right to demand that the worship leader conduct a style of worship that always meets my needs. Alternatively, the more willing I am to be part of a worship experience that does not work to meet the needs of one specific cultural grouping, the more my spiritual experience is broadened and enhanced. There may be some aspects of worship that I like and that meet my spiritual needs, and there may be some that I could do without. As different cultural groupings share their traditions of worship, I learn new ways to enhance my own spiritual development. By being willing to try different worship styles, I might discover a cultural ritual or tradition that I might not have anticipated that I would like.

One side note: When we began changing the style of worship, we were afraid that the elder persons in the church, i.e., the little old ladies, would object to the contemporary music. But they really enjoyed it and even swayed with the music. This surprised not only us but them. Now when they are in the community and someone says, "You go to that church where they play that loud rock music. Don't you hate it? I would." They respond, "I thought I would hate it, too, but I love it!" They turned out to be among the church's best evangelists.

Plague # 3: *An Inward Focus*

A few years ago the church prepared to adopt a sister church that had fifteen people in worship. In the past, this church had been unwilling to change their style of worship, but now they felt they had reached a point of desperation and had an openness to do whatever it takes. Their most recent pastor had resigned, and they did not have the money to call another one. I had been a friend to the previous pastor, and the members knew me; therefore, I had an in with them. The plan was that members from our church would come in and assist in leading worship (at a time other than Sunday morning), and the music would be provided by our Praise Band until we could help them develop their own music program. We agreed upon a time limit of one year or until the church averaged one hundred in attendance, whichever came first. In return, we expected nothing monetary, but we did expect that it would shift our church's inward focus to an external one.

Sure enough, people in our church responded, "We should take care of our own church rather than another one." Such thinking reflected our inward focus. Others were concerned about what would happen when they couldn't reach the pastor because the pastor was doing something for that other church. Gradually, the focus shifted to: "If we are willing to go door-to-door and do evangelism for our sister church, why don't we do that for our own church?" The very things that we were excited about doing for another church were things that we might have been doing in our community. The planning of this mission project helped us to see that our inward focus was preventing us from evangelizing in our own neighborhood.[5]

When a person is dying, they often become self-absorbed. In dying churches, the process of turning inward to comfort is the quickest way to its death. A church that is sick and in pain grasps at anything for immediate relief; any quick fix to alleviate its present condition will do. In its quest for self-preservation, it clings to the familiar. It does not have energy to meet new people and begin new life. Ezekiel's image of the valley of dry bones (chapter 38) is an apt image of the present state of the church. The focalization is on itself and its own problems. It cannot see that by putting its own problems aside and helping someone else, it might alleviate its own pain.

One of my colleagues recently shared with me that the dominant group in his church was constantly harassing him; always finding fault and claiming that he was doing a poor job as pastor. The church had a history of chewing up pastors, and those who would not tolerate the abuse ended up leaving. Those who didn't eventually got fired. The church's attendance numbers were dwindling, finances were a major source of tension, and morale was low. Any energy it had to sustain itself was spent campaigning to get rid of the pastor. Telephone calls, e-mails, and secret meetings at parishioners' homes not only sustained the power of the dominant group but seemed to create energy onto itself. (Some churches thrive on conflict.) He asked me if I had any suggestions.

I suggested that he bottle that energy and redirect it outside of the church. A pastor will not be able to suppress that energy, and he or she shouldn't seek to disable it because it is all the church has left. Instead, he looked for a mission project outside of the church for them to become involved. The community was adamant against allowing a home for battered women to come into its neighborhood. The church discussed the matter and determined that they disagreed with the community and that the home was providing a community service that they should support. The church members worked day and night trying to get the community to come around and do the right thing. The last I heard, they had successfully managed to get the proposal passed at a town meeting. Regretfully, some members were still as bitter and angry as when they were inwardly focused. Fortunately, however, the pastor had managed to use their energy and rechannel it into something that they could feel good about.

It is the goal of the multicultural church to teach new patterns of relating and practicing rules for interaction (see chapter 5). The multicultural church provides a safe and controlled environment (its leaders hold individuals accountable for their behavior) to develop relationships with persons from culturally diverse groupings. There is a sense of trust that if prejudice arises, it will be confronted in a caring atmosphere.

Rick Rusaw and Eric Swanson state that for a church to be inwardly strong, it needs to be externally focused.[6] To minister to the congregation is to equip them to be ministers in the community. The more the ministers reach out and transform the community, the focus shifts from inward problems to responsibility to care for the outward environment. It became our mission to teach peace and enact justice to the community of Randolph.

Plague # 4: *Low Commitment*

As a seminarian, I heard stories about how ministers were supposed to work eighty hours a week. I worried about balancing a career with marriage and children (which I had planned to do). I understood that a "good pastor" was an overworked pastor. I wondered what message this sent to the congregation as a pastor boasted about working all those hours and at the same time preached about the importance of spending time with family.

My theory is that pastors who feel powerless in other areas of their lives or who do not receive much affirmation outside of the church spend their lives wrapped up in being the pastor. The role of pastor comes with power and authority, and when one is functioning as the pastor, one feels powerful. Pastors are beloved when they are continually accessible to parishioners. They are at every meeting and have their hand in every project. They perceive they are modeling a high commitment to the church, but in actuality they are overfunctioning. And in pastor-parish relationships, an overfunctioning pastor only leaves room for the church to underfunction. Symptoms of underfunctioning congregations include, but are not limited to, low involvement, sporadic attendance, inability to meet the budget, and criticism directed toward the pastor.

There is a direct correlation between overfunctioning pastors and underfunctioning congregations that produces a sense of low commitment, which is why congregations enable pastors to overfunction. Parishioners are not encouraged to discern their own gifts for ministry because the beloved pastor needs to do them in order to feel affirmed. For every psychological reason that the pastor needs to be the pastor, e.g., to feel good about his or her ministry and ability to make a difference in the world, is the same reason that people become active in the life of a church. Underutilized gifts eventually become like dry bones. They get caught in a cycle that sees that the church ministry as the pastor's job.

I will address this issue in chapter 6, but I will mention here that when a pastor overfunctions, he or she is modeling to the congregation that it is acceptable, even desirable, to hoard power. Power equals participation in the congregation, and those who participate more tend to receive more power. The overfunctioning pastor is collecting more than his or her share of power that is needed to function. A pastor, who is a multicultural leader working to make a shift in power from the dominant group to the marginalized group, needs to make a shift in his or her own power from the pastorate to the congregation.

Plague #5: *A Closed System*

Recently while my husband and I were on vacation, we attended a United Church of Christ in another state. It had been a long time since I was in an unfamiliar church that didn't know I was a pastor. We entered through the Fellowship Hall as one or two people caught our eye and said "Hi," although not very enthusiastically. They looked rather unsettled by our presence. We made our way up to the sanctuary (it was confusing as to which way we were supposed to go) and decided to sit in a pew close to the front. We soon realized we were more than fifteen minutes early and had plenty of time to adjust to our new surroundings.

We watched while parishioners entered the sanctuary. Consistently, each would see us and look away or look for someone they knew. Some smiled as they approached us, but no one asked us our name or whether we were new to the community (this was not a vacation spot) or showed any interest in us, other than we seemed to be causing some anxiety. Eventually about fifty people came into the sanctuary and greeted each other with a hug and a kind word. We noticed that while they talked, there was often a look of deep concern for the person speaking.

My husband and I could not have felt more uncomfortable. I describe the experience like this: *It felt like we were sitting in someone else's living room as an uninvited guest.* In retrospect, I think they were dramatically trying to show us how close knit they all were, perhaps as a sign of their friendliness. But it had a paradoxical effect. My perception was that this close-knit community was closed off from allowing anyone else to enter its midst. My husband and I are both white middle-class heterosexual people. What would it have been like for a Hispanic American couple, or a gay or lesbian couple?

Segregated European American churches also appear as closed systems when they use an internally coded language. The pastor refers to something that happened months ago and everyone laughs as they recall that event. Or the worship leader comments, "Everyone knows that I don't usually cook . . ." and everyone laughs. They are inside jokes. The bulletin has an asterisk (*) next to the hymn but no code as to what that means. I remember when one of our students was going to run a workshop for visitors. She announced that they were to meet her in the narthex. No one showed up because the visitors were unfamiliar with the term "narthex." Church members need to view their churches as public spaces and not closed systems. They should make every effort to imagine what it would be like if they had never visited a church before in their life. How difficult would it be to adhere to the etiquette of what was expected of one on Sunday morning?

Plague #6: *Anxiety About Evangelism*

In segregated European American communities, we do not invite friends and family to church because we are afraid of being pushy. One of the parishioners related a story about how he would golf with a friend every Saturday, and every time they planned this outing on the phone, his friend would ask, "How about golfing on Sunday?" The parishioner would always respond, "Now, you know I always go to church on Sunday." This went on for some time until the parishioner couldn't take it any more and said, "You always invite me to golf with you on Sunday and I always tell you I can't because I go to church on Sunday." And the friend responded, "I know, I was hoping you would invite me to go to church with you."

Segregated European American communities are not excited about what is happening at their church, so it does not occur to them to invite others. There doesn't seem like there is anything to share. When attendance seems sparse and money is an issue, .it makes it difficult to invite someone to attend worship. We want to create a good first impression; if we fear that is not going to happen, then we don't bother to invite them.

There are three phases of evangelism: A to B, B to C, and C to D. The first, A to B, involves getting people out of bed on Sunday morning and picking them up and driving them to church. Studies show that most people visit a church because someone invited them. The invited tend to become high-commitment parishioners. Because they were invited by someone, they tend to be good evangelists who go out and invite others. This is perhaps the most crucial phase of evangelism–and the most neglected–in the segregated European American church.

The second phase, B to C, is getting visitors to come back a second time. Visitors will assess the Christian Education program and youth programs if they have children; the relevance of the sermon to daily life; whether the church has air conditioning, etc. But most importantly, visitors need to sense the presence of God in the church. Is the service Christ-centered? Does the Holy Spirit dance, and is spontaneity warmly welcomed into the order of worship? Does the choir sing as if they actually believe what they are singing and believe that it is their calling to try to persuade the congregation to believe?

Most European American congregations perceive that they are effectively evangelizing from B to C. They describe themselves as "warm and friendly." (I have yet to visit a church that thinks it's "cold and unfriendly.") Evangelism means saying hello to someone you think you saw in worship last week. The disadvantage in a numerically large church is that people are unsure whether another person is a visitor. They are afraid to say anything to someone they don't know for fear that the other person will get angry and say, "I've been coming to this church for ten years!" I make it a point to teach people to introduce themselves to anyone they meet whom they do not know. I also teach people to say, "It's nice to see you," rather than "It's nice to meet you" and have someone respond, "We've met before."

The third phase is C to D, or a visitor who continures to attend and wants to become an active church member. This phase has almost nothing to do with how much they like the minister, enjoy the church service, or come to experience the Trinity. It has everything to do with whether there is a space for them within the church. If the perception is that there is nothing to do, no opportunities for ministry and mission, and that the power is held by a few individuals and not shared evenly, a visitor will not likely continue attending that church.

Summary

I began by differentiating the segregated white church from other segregated churches with one ethnic grouping whose mission is to preserve their cultural identity. Most European Americans have lost touch with their ethnic background, yet continue to sustain white churches. In this chapter, I have identified six plagues that are afflicting the segregated European American church. These plagues are causing affliction to members of the congregation who were previously quite comfortable. The afflictions are a direct result of the church's segregated status. The church needs to admit they have a problem and foresee that the problem can be alleviated by seeking a different way of functioning. The most significant change is that the dominant group needs to share its power with marginalized groups. These plagues are an indication that God is calling the church to change.

CHAPTER TWO

Parting the Red Sea

*Leadership Empowerment for the
Multicultural Movement*

WHEN I WAS IN THE FIFTH GRADE, I decided I wanted to play the trombone. After returning to school with a signed parental form, I was called down to the principal's office and informed that a mistake had been made: When asked, "Which instrument would you like to play?" I checked the trombone. The school officials explained to me that "little girls don't play the trombone." They suggested that I learn the flute instead. As I had been taught to respect authority figures, I politely explained that I had discussed this with my parents and had chosen the trombone. I don't remember where I summoned the strength to stand firm in my decision, but by the grace of God I did. I learned to play the trombone, and I played that instrument through college. So in the 1980s, early on in my ministry, when people would say to me, "I didn't think women could be ministers," it was a familiar chant. I believe that God wanted me to play the trombone and, as one of the things I needed to do to prepare for being a pastor in a traditionally male profession, confront prejudice.

Historically, the pattern of confronting prejudice goes like this: the marginalized group is expected to confront the dominant group. When people are in a situation in which they have been denied access to power, they are the ones who lead the protest. In the African American community, prophets such as Martin Luther King, Jr., made an historic "I Have A Dream" speech in Washington and united persons of color and European Americans. But the initial protest began because Rosa Parks was challenged to give up her seat to a white person. Because the African American was being marginalized by the European American, it was the African American community that led the confrontation. But not all marginalized groups will have a spokesperson emerge to challenge the dominant group. In this chapter, I will offer strategies to empower multicultural leaders from either the dominant or marginalized groups to unite together in solidarity and find ways to distribute power equally. I will propose that a person does not have to be a member of a particular marginalized group in order to advocate on their behalf.

Thus, when contemporary multicultural leaders ask the question, "Who should confront the dominant group?" our answer is much different than the one we would have given in the past. Today, if a young girl was told she was not allowed to learn how to play the trombone because of her gender, we would be talking about a lawsuit. While the court might take a statement of her experience, she would not be the prosecuting attorney in the case. We would hire an attorney well versed in the legal ramifications of sexual discrimination and expect that he would be a spokesperson for her civil rights. This illustration represents a significant shift in the way we confront oppression. No longer do we empower the oppressed to present their case to convince the oppressor to stop oppressing. Contemporary models now advocate that those in the dominant group who are ethically and culturally sensitive confront others in the dominant group who are not. While the marginalized group should be included as part of the process, and as the shift in power takes place, they will emerge as multicultural leaders and should not be unfairly placed in the position of confronting the dominant group.

Who Should be the Leaders?

I would think it virtually impossible to become a multicultural church if the pastor does not feel called to participate in the movement as a spiritual leader. The pastor has a significant role to play in the process. He or she is responsible for articulating a theological vision of the multicultural movement. The pastor listens intentionally to his or her parishioners and frames their call into theological language that speaks to the rest of the congregation. Because he or she is seminary trained, the pastor can help the leaders find biblical passages that help attach the vision to biblical stories. God intervenes in the Bible, often in predicable, consistent ways. By discerning these ways, the pastor can point to the ways that God is intervening again to encourage a church to become multicultural.

One evening while I was at the church, I had a vision. Set before my eyes was Noah's Ark. Like most traditional New England–style church buildings, the architecture of the church in Randolph contains a ceiling that is rounded to mirror the bottom of Noah's Ark. It symbolizes that parishioners are poured out into the pews and "saved." Since the days of my Sunday school education, I had been taught that Noah was a biblical model of faith because he followed what God wanted him to do–that is, Noah built an ark and saved himself and his relatives from a horrific flood. But, for the first time, I wondered how the people who were drowning around Noah and his family might have felt. What was the perspective on this story? Did they cry out to be saved as they were drowning before the ark? What was the dialogue inside of the ark? Could they hear the cries of the people and, if they could, did they try to ignore them? How relevant is this vision to the current state of the Christian church?

Because we knew that people in our community preceived the church as a closed system. We had not thought about how that translated into our community. Perhaps we had a neighbor who was waiting for an invitation to come to church, or one who was aching to be heard in her pain and suffering. As I began to prayerfully listen to those cries, I heard them say that, in their perception, the church was a locked, secure building and that they felt excluded. One Saturday a few of us simply stood out in front of the local supermarket, passing out pamphlets about the church and just asking people what they had heard about it. The findings surprised us: Most people knew where the church was located but could not think of one activity that the church was doing in the community.

So I gathered a group of people in the church who I knew could also see the vision before us. Initially, I drew equally from the dominant and marginalized groups in the church (as best as I could determine who would be in which group; most people fall into both groups due to the fact that each individual is an amalgamation of many cultural groupings, some dominant, some marginalized). I tried to draw from as many cultural groupings as I perceived were in the church at the time and gather them together merely to discuss our presence as a church in the community. This initial group included a broad range of ages, economic situations, abilities, etc.

This group was not static, and people were included for as long as they felt they had something to contribute. The group was characterized by its fluidity: People easily shifted in and out of it. As time went on, the discussion turned from identifying what was not working to how we might implement something that might work more effectively. The major issue was being a visible presence in the community, but because the church membership was largely European American, that soon changed to enabling the church to more visibly reflect the changing demographics of the community.

What made this group different from others was the way it functioned. People were asked to be involved while others just showed up. Some had long histories of being involved with the church, while others were new to the church. We explained that we had invited certain members because they had a specific skill or personality characteristic that we thought would be valuable to the project. Factors such as length of membership, pledging ability, etc., were not considered predictors of performance. We also selected people who had the ability to identify others with certain skills and gifts. The task force (as it was known early on) merely functioned to identify who in the church could do what needed to be done. The group was also responsible for building confidence, lending support, and affirming when tasks were done well. These are the people who became leaders in the multicultural movement.

Due to the plague of declining membership, some people perceive that they are being asked to participate because "they couldn't find anyone else." We tried to be sensitive to this dynamic and thus we did not ask marginalized persons to do a task that could potentially be seen as undesirable. It was important to make sure that everyone had equal opportunity to do tasks that had some prestige attached to them, rather than the ones that were equivalent to taking out the trash.

We also found that there are cultural differences in the ways people should be asked to participate as leaders. If a leader in the church asked a European American to do a specific task or serve on a committee, that person has the option to say "yes" or "no." They perceive that their answer has no bearing on their continued relationship with the person who asked them. But some cultural groupings perceive that if a powerful member of the church, such as the pastor or a member of the dominant group, asks them to do something, that there is only one answer: "yes."

Some cultural groupings perceive that if one who is in a position of power asks them to participate, then it is a great honor since it communicates that the person doing the asking recognizes that the person being asked is competent in the task. It would be an insult to the person doing the asking to say "no" because that would convey that the person doing the asking is wrong about is or her choice. Thus, they might not give an answer at all, assuming that if asked, one should be willing to do the task. In multicultural churches, to be asked to do something—to participate on a task force or serve on a committee—is considered an honor. Too often in segregated churches, when someone is asked to serve on a committee, that person sighs and says, "Couldn't you find anyone else?"

Multicultural leaders, in summary, are those who are particularly skilled at identifying not only their own gifts but those of others as well, building confidence in the person whom they engage in the process. This group of leaders represents each of the cultural groupings listed in our definition so that every member of the congregation perceives that his or her cultural groupings participate in the decision making and other manifestations of power. The objective is to involve everyone as the prophet Joel predicted. "Then afterward, I will pour out my spirit of all flesh; your sons and your daughters shall prophecy, your old men shall dream dreams and your young men shall see visions. Even on the male and female slaves, in those days, I will pour out my spirit" (2:28–29). Multicultural leaders perceive that each person has a gift to share in the multicultural movement, a gift that has been poured out by the spirit. Discerning those gifts primarily is the task of multicultural leaders.

Strategies for Multicultural Leaders

I will offer three strategies for leaders to equip themselves for the multicultural movement. Foremost, the leaders must genuinely believe that God is calling them as leaders and that they have been blessed with the gift of leadership that will move the process along. The leaders must be encouraged to see God's guidance when the path becomes difficult to navigate or simply overwhelming. Most importantly, these people must be perceived by the followers as people who are living out their faith and engaging in these tasks because they believe that this is what God wants them to be doing. As a faith community, we continually witnessed that the movement toward multiculturalism is God's vision for us.

The first strategy is that *multicultural leaders bear witness to their own experience of marginality.* This strategy is one of confrontation to convince the dominant group to share their power with the marginalized group. As Moses had to convince Pharaoh to let go of his power in order to allow the Israelites to cross the Reed Sea, much of which multicultural leaders do is to persuade those who are in power that it is in everyone's best interests to redistribute that power more equally.

When I was searching for a church to serve as pastor, there were search committees that saw "Rev. Laurene Bowers" and corrected the mistake by inserting a *c* in between the *n* and the final *e* in order for it to read "Laurence." It became enough of an issue that I had to circulate my profile as "Rev. Laurene Beth Bowers" to avoid that awkward moment when I arrived for the interview with the search committee and they looked disappointed. If you call the church and ask for "Rev. Laurence Bowers," my secretary will say, "There's nobody here by that name."

Initially, we perceived that individuals could be categorized as either being in the dominant or marginalized group, yet we soon realized that almost all people have affiliations with both groups. For instance, I am a European American who identifies with the dominant group culture, but I am also a woman who identifies with the marginalized group. African American men identify with the dominant culture of gender but also identify with the marginalized group with respect to ethnicity. Most European American men have had an experience of being judged because of a physical or birth characteristic. Men who are short in stature are less likely to be hired than men who are tall. A man once shared with me that he lost his job because of his gray hair. The company thought that he was not presenting "a youthful image" to their clientele.

As we stood before the Reed Sea, praying that a miracle would happen so that we could escape from oppression into unknown, never-explored-before territory, we had to do some convincing about who was coming with us and why they should join us. The multicultural leaders witnessed to their own experience of being marginalized, and others in the congregation began to identify with these experiences and to realize that the way in which we distribute power was oppressive and therefore wrong. They spoke of what it is like to feel powerless, to be treated unfairly and judged by one's appearance. When we perceive that we are being judged negatively, it often renders us helpless. In order to cope with this feeling, some people will victimize others. By passing the pain of helplessness, one feels more powerful, even though that sensation lasts only as long as it takes to commit this act of victimization. Parishioners gained insight into these dynamics of violence and victimization and began to see more clearly the negative effects of the functioning of our congregation.

Once individuals are in touch with their history of feeling powerless, they are less likely to hoard power. This is especially true for those who have histories of being sexually abused. This form of victimization renders the victim in such a helpless state that he or she may spend his or her whole life trying to gain enough power to "never have that feeling again." They enter into church settings, however, and they want to control everything that happens. They become "control freaks": Some fear that everything that happens is their fault, so they try to control every cause and effect. Thus, redistributing power can be a way to help victims heal their experience of victimization. Even though they did not have power to control their perpetrator's behavior, they no longer need to control everyone around them for fear of further victimization.

I have seen this dynamic occur for cultural reasons as well. Those who have experienced prejudice may inadvertently pass that pain onto others by being prejudiced against another marginal grouping. This often takes the focus off of their own cultural grouping, especially if it is a current target of prejudice. As mentioned in the introduction, marginalized cultural groupings tend to be prejudiced against one another because they have to compete for what little power is available from the dominant group. By witnessing to experiences of prejudice, we found that people began to understand that the dominant group was enabling this dynamic by hoarding power.

Multicultural leaders share their own experiences of being marginalized to help others connect with their own. I call this dynamic "a point of identification." Effective leaders share their experience of marginality as a point of identification with those who have also been marginalized. This reinforces the equality of all persons, even though there are clearly some people who perceive that they have a right to more power than others. By helping those in the dominant group to identify their point of identification with the marginalized group, they develop empathy for what it is like to be marginalized. They then realize that hoarding power is an unjust thing to do. Jesus commands that we treat other people the way that we would want to be treated. When the multicultural leader asks, "How did you feel when you were treated that way?" and one in the dominant group responds, "I didn't like it," then the multicultural leaders says, "Now you know what it must be like for the marginalized person."

When God began parting the Reed Sea, not everyone thought every other cultural grouping should be allowed to cross. Multicultural leaders had to convince others that it was an "all or none" journey. Whereas becoming a multicultural church involves *every* member, becoming the multicultural church involves *every* church. If we exclude one cultural grouping, such as the GLBT community, then we will not be allowed into the promised land. This is at the core of what we believe as a faith community. It is also the premise of this book.

The second strategy for multicultural leaders is *to advocate for a cultural grouping with which they do not identify*. Moses identified with both the Israelites (the marginalized group) and the Egyptians (who are perceived by the Israelites as the dominant group). As an Egyptian living presumably in power and prestige, Moses witnesses an Egyptian man beating a Hebrew man. He comes to the defense of the Hebrew man by killing the Egyptian (Exod. 2:11–12). Rahab, a Canaanite woman living on the edge of the land of Canaan, is willing to assist the Israelites by hiding the spies from the Canaanite authorities (Josh. 2). Both biblical characters are viewed as examples of faith by the author of Hebrews (11:25, 31). Both advocate for a marginalized group with which they have no previous connection. (We assume that Moses doesn't yet know he has a connection to the Israelites.)

As a woman who has experienced marginality, I have passion for promoting the rights of women—especially to convince churches to accept women in the ministry. I have spent the last twenty years serving four churches in the United Church of Christ as "the first female pastor." I personally benefit because it makes it easier for me to find a church to serve. I also receive personal satisfaction from being a forerunner, knowing that my efforts will make it easier for the women who follow me. Most advocates who work toward promoting the rights of the marginalized have an affiliation with the cultural grouping whom they represent. A *good* leader advocates on behalf of his or her own cultural grouping in order to promote their interests and attain power.

But the Bible teaches us that a *great* leader advocates on behalf of a cultural grouping not of his or her own. When I speak on behalf of the GLBT community, someone will ask, "Is someone in your family gay?" "Why are you speaking about a marginalized group that you know nothing about?" Honestly, I have no idea why God would want me to be an advocate for the GLBT community as a heterosexual woman. But I know this for sure: I have been appointed by God to be a spokesperson to the dominant culture of heterosexuals, to challenge their prejudices against the GLBT community.

The third strategy is *for multicultural leaders to encourage and support each other*. In the way we constructed the process, we risked that some multicultural leaders would emerge more powerful than others. As a microcosm of the larger system, it became clear that multicultural leaders had to model the equal distribution of power. When there was disagreement among them, which was considered part of the course, it was agreed upon how they would disagree. Rather than attacking someone's faith or personhood, we set guidelines for what would constitute a healthy disagreement.

Multicultural leaders also learned how to offer words of affirmation. Instead of focusing on what was not going right, we tried to keep the energy positive and focus on every sign and wonder that seemed to be pointing us closer to the promised land. We continually emphasized that this journey was not a journey toward collecting persons to become a numerically larger church, but a spiritual journey to become more faithful Christians. We then witnessed to these signs along the way that we believe showed us that God was the true leader of the movement and was revealing to us the direction that we were to take. Sometimes we complained that we didn't know which way to go, and then we would stop and offer prayer for one another.

The dominant group became convinced that they needed to let go of their power and share it with the marginalized group because they were convinced that we were all headed for the promised land. They came to accept that we cannot draw boundaries around one cultural grouping and exclude that group from the journey. They were convinced by multicultural leaders, who helped them to recognize a point of identification with the marginalized group.

When we praise the gifts given to them by God, we praise God. Multicultural leaders also model self-care for the congregation. People who are encouraged to take care of themselves will then be able to be a loving, caring presence for the congregation.

CHAPTER THREE

The Burning Bush

Multicultural Images of God

During confirmation class, one of the youths asked, "Why do all the paintings of Jesus in the church portray him as white?" I stood stunned for a moment. "Was Jesus white?" the class asked curiously. It seemed to go against the grain of everything I had taught them about imaging the divine. The class immediately went on a field trip around the church to survey the ethnic background of Jesus as projected in our paintings. As we traveled, we invited the adults we met along the way to join us. It was an accurate observation: Every painting in the church depicted Jesus as a white American male. After several years of working to become a multicultural church, we had learned a valuable lesson about the way in which churches maintain the dominant group's power through its image of God in Jesus.

Like many churches, we had purchased a series of Warner Sallman's prints that portrayed Jesus. Some fifty years ago, Sallman painted a series of paintings showing Jesus in several biblical scenes, such as in the garden, knocking on the door, etc. Most American Christians would be able to identify Stallman's famous portrait of Jesus. It is the familiar picture of a Jesus with long, brown, wavy hair. Modern painters have helped us to image the divine through their own projections. Therefore, artists tend to image Jesus as a likeness of themselves. They paint portraits of Jesus that reflect their own ethnic background. Sallman's image of what Jesus might look like is ingrained in our minds as what Jesus must have looked like because of the popularity of these paintings. Jesus, however, was born into a

Palestinian family and probably had dark skin and short, wavy hair.

Sunday school curriculum has also promoted the power of the dominant group. I remember reading a book about all the biblical heroes of the Old Testament, all of whom were men. Pastors, too, were pictured as men. To a girl growing up in the church in the 1960s, it reinforced the question of whether women could be ministers. The curriculum portrayed all the children around Jesus as white. The curriculum was not intentionally feeding prejudice and the superiority of the European Americans, but nevertheless it had a powerful impact not only on the way we perceive other cultural groupings but also in the way we image the divine.

Freud asserted that the divine was nothing more than a projection that originates within our own mind.[1] This dynamic led him to conclude that God is nothing more than what human beings "image" God to be. Even though this psychological dynamic is operating in our imaging of the divine, it neither denies nor confirms the existence of God. The portrayal of the divine as anthropomorphic is prevalent in the Bible. In Genesis, for example, God is said to be walking around in the cool of the breeze in the garden (3:8). In Christianity, the Word is made flesh in the person of Jesus Christ (John 1:14) to facilitate our faith so that we may desire to develop a relationship with the divine. Imaging the divine to look like ourselves is a human tendency and one that a multicultural church does not need to suppress. We can all appreciate that there are others who are also created in the image of God.

Biblical Images of the Divine

The book of Genesis commissions us to image human beings as a reflection of the divine. "So God created humankind in his image, in the image of God he created them, male and female he created them" (1:27). God created us "in his image," emphasizes that we are like God in our abilities, talents, and gifts. These gifts equip and empower us to be instruments to bestow divine blessings on others. Phyllis Trible observes that if God creates human beings to be male and female as a reflection of the divine image, then God must embody both male and female attributes.[2]

In the Bible, opposing word pairs are juxtaposed as a literary device to convey "everything else in-between."[3] When Genesis 1:27 employs the word pair "male and female," it is the Bible's way of including all persons with respect to race, ethnicity, gender, sexual orientation, class, ability, and age. Therefore, there is no cultural grouping that is excluded from God's image. God's attributes not only include those that we associate with as being either male or female but also all the characteristics, and abilities in the range of the human race.

Moses effectively led the Jews to the promised land because he was able to imagine that God could appear in any number of images. (In the ancient world, God was often viewed in terms of nature or storm imagery[4]). Moses was even able to see the presence of God in a burning bush. In the ancient world, there was a belief that if one sees the face of God, one would die. Moses was cautious to not look upon the face of God. This belief might have functioned to deflect the Israelites' attention from beholding the face and looking for the revelation of God's presence in other places.

In the New Testament, God, the Word, becomes flesh in the person of Jesus Christ. Since the incarnation was in the body of a male, Christians associate God with being male. We image God as we image Jesus. God had a tough enough time getting the ancient world to believe in God; how much more challenging would it have been had God appeared as a woman! The message we take is that God is imaged as a male. This misses the point of salvation history. Instead of seeing the larger picture, we have accepted a small detail as gospel.

In this chapter, I will examine the image of God projected and promoted in segregated churches. To become a multicultural church, congregations need to broaden our images of God to be inclusive of all cultural groupings.

The Image of the Divine in Segregated European American Churches

In segregated European American churches, God is portrayed with the attributes of the dominant group, i.e., an elderly white man with a gray beard sitting on a throne. David Anderson observes that even the act of sitting projects power.[5] Judges sit, and everyone in the courtroom stands when they enter. When Rosa Parks decided not to give up her seat on a segregated bus in Alabama, she asserted her power to protest against a racist practice. Parishioners will not sit down in the pews until the pastor begins a descent into the chair. The image of God "sitting in the throne" reflects the customs and traditions that American culture associates with those who have power—namely, the dominant group.

But where does the image of an elderly white man with a gray beard come from? I suspect that this traditional image of the divine relates to the myth of Santa Claus. A popular icon in his own right, Santa promises presents as a reward for good behavior. Familiar stories say that those who behave badly would get coal in their Christmas stocking. The image of Santa is readily reinforced: One asks for presents, and within a few weeks they are received. God's promise of salvation is otherworldly. In many instances, Santa Claus mythology has become entangled with Christian theology. When individuals experience trauma, they may wonder, "Is God punishing me for something I did wrong?" My response is, "Do you mean like getting coal in your stocking?"

With our current awareness of the dynamics of sexual abuse, we should have a problem in promoting a myth in which young children are encouraged to sit on the lap of an elderly man to request gifts. We should also find it problematic that a man would be allowed unlimited access to the home of children in such a way that no one is supposed to see him. If at the age of ten I became aware that my parents were lying about Santa, then might I, at the age of twenty, become aware that my parents and the pastor were lying about God? We need to reevaluate all of the traditional ways in which we teach our children to image dominance.

Christians believe that God is all powerful, and so we image God with the same characteristics and attributes as the dominant group. This serves also to reinforce the power of the dominant group. Therefore, they have an investment to sustain this image. When I challenged the notion that God's attributes were not exclusively masculine–e.g., a strong, fatherly figure who meters out punishment for misbehavior—and introduced feminine attributes—e.g., a nurturing, caring, motherly figure whose loving embrace comforts us in our moment of need–some perceived me as being blasphemous.

The problem is that European Americans tend to have a narrow and limited view of what God looks like and who God is. I suggest that this limitation is one of the primary causes of Plague #2, Spiritual Boredom. One of the reasons why people come to church is to see God. Christians believe that we see Jesus through the faces of one another. If we only see white European Americans on Sunday morning, we see a very limited view of the divine. Further, Generation X and Millennials are bored with this traditional image of the divine, which supports the interests of the dominant group. Society is more diverse and sophisticated. Many are moving away from a need to promote these traditional images–images that sustain the power of one group over another. Generation X and Millennials are looking for fresh images of the divine that meet contemporary needs.

At the same time, I am not advocating that people suppress their beloved image of God as a "white elderly man with a gray beard." The approach to become a multicultural church is not to subtract who we are and what we believe, but rather to add to who and what we are. We are building the realm of God, not taking it down brick by brick. If the reader believes that this image enhances his or her spirituality, so be it. I, however, am arguing for us to appreciate that this image might not be everybody's image of God; nor should it be. Instead of cringing when the pastor uses language and imagery other than what is traditionally used to refer to the divine, we should practice tolerance and open our hearts and minds to new revelations of God.

The Cultural Background of Pastors

One Sunday morning as I processed down the sanctuary aisle, a little girl standing on the edge of a pew pointed to me and in a loud voice inquired, "Mommy, is that God?" Smiling, I turned around and said to the congregation, "How wonderful! This young girl is able to image God as female because she has only known a female pastor."

Our image of God is also derived from our relationship with the pastor.

Pastors function as representatives of God. When a pastor enters a hospital room and the family says, "Thank God, the pastor is here," they perceive that the pastor's presence invokes the divine's presence. Because we cannot see God, and because God's intervention is often orchestrated through God's children, we come to know God in and through one another. As the pastor preaches the sermon, officiates at baptisms, weddings, and funerals, he or she is a public image of power who helps people develop a relationship with God by way of developing a relationship with the pastor.

As children, our earliest images of caregivers are formed through our relationship with parents. When children feel cared for by their parents, they are more likely to feel cared for by others, and they can develop trust. Ana-Maria Rizzuto, in her classic book *The Birth of the Living God,* illustrates the process by which parental images are transferred to form images of the divine.[6] The care-giving that we experience in our relationship with our parents also allows us to transfer our expectations of how others will care for us, and will also be transferred onto "pastors." It is often noted that without a human experience of care-giving, we would be unable to understand what it means when we say, "Jesus loves me."

It follows that one's relationship with the pastor facilitates one's relationship with God. Therefore, the cultural background of the pastor is instrumental to the development of one's image of God. If the pastor is an African American male, parishioners might image God as an African American male. If the pastor is an Asian American female, parishioners might image God as an Asian American female. If the pastor is a European American male, parishioners will image God as a European American male. There are certainly some exceptions to this dynamic. Often African American churches will image God as a European American male because we tend to associate God with the dominant cultures as outlined above.

To test this dynamic and to see it working, ask a confirmation class to describe what God looks like. Some might identify physical characteristics and emotional attributes of the current and previous pastors.

For instance, when I asked the confirmation class to describe God, they said that they used to think that God was a man, but now they think that God is more like a woman. They used to picture God as old, but now they picture God as middle-aged but "cool." One youth spoke about how God has long, brown, wavy hair and is short in stature. They said that God is easy to talk to and approachable. God is caring and nurturing. The kids seemed to be genuinely unaware that they were contrasting the previous pastor with their current one. It is not a coincidence that I have long brown hair, am middle-aged, and, I may add, "cool."

Members of the same church have a history of interacting with the same pastors, so they have what I call "a collective image of God." If you ask long-term members to describe God, they will not only use similar images, but similar themes will emerge when discussing what they believe God does.

European American churches select pastors who fit their traditional image of God and who are of the same cultural grouping as this collective image. Historically, most European American churches have been served exclusively by European American men; most churches work to sustain this image as the one it projects to the community. When a church calls only a European American man as its pastor and spiritual leader, it projects to the community that this is the image of God worshiped in that church. If the church is journeying toward multiculturalism, a projection of such an image is counterproductive to any strategy it implements. Projecting a more inclusive image of God to the community is one of the most important strategies in becoming a multicultural church.

Today, the number of women ministers is increasing. Churches that have been and continue to be exclusively served by male pastors are clinging to the European American male image of God and limiting their experience of God. (This also contributes to projecting the image of an outdated church to the community.) At this point in history, when I encounter a church that has never been served by a female pastor, I want to know, why not? What has been the dialogue among search committee members that has excluded this population of available pastors? These churches are setting themselves up as red flags whereby the collective image sustains the dominant group and the church practices prejudice.

Churches have the right and responsibility to call as their spiritual leaders any pastor whom they want. Today, however, churches that continue to call pastors who fit this collective image are also limiting their experience of God. Calling a pastor who fits this collective image can also be a recipe for conflict. I recently heard about a church who called a pastor because he looked like one of their beloved former pastors. Everything went along fine as long as he looked and behaved like the former pastor. But as soon as he began to assert his individuality and did things differently, he forced the church to test their projection. Initially the church loved him because he invoked feelings that they had toward the previous pastor. However, when he showed signs of not being the previous pastor, people thought he was doing things wrong.

At my church, we have an ethnically, culturally, and sexually diverse staff. We have an African American male pastor who was ordained as an African Methodist Episcopal minister; an African American female pastor who is in-care with the American Baptist Conference; a Chinese American pastor who is ordained Lutheran; and an openly lesbian woman who is in-care with the United Church of Christ. I recently received a phone call from a Hispanic American pastor who had heard about our church. He called to inquire whether we had any openings for a pastor. Parishioners will tell you that since we have journeyed toward multiculturalism, their spirituality has increased and they have a fuller image of who God is. Likewise, they perceive they feel closer and know God better. A Jamaican American woman recently said to me, "When I first started attending this church, I thought that God was an old white man, but now I think of God as a rainbow of ethnic colors who embodies the best of male and female qualities. I feel like I know God."

Language and Other Mediums of Imagery

Most of us grew up listening to worship and spiritual leaders referring to God as "he." The Hebrew Bible and the New Testament uses a masculine singular verb to refer to God's activity, and we refer to God in the masculine singular. Using the masculine pronoun sustains the traditional image of God and also works to sustain the power of the dominant group (with respect to gender).

A church that is prayerfully moving to become multicultural and also shifting its power from the dominant group to an equal distribution amongst the congregation, needs to carefully evaluate the language and imagery it uses when referring to God. Language is one of the primary mediums of imagery. If a child comes to church and sees a male God imaged in the curriculum, and hears the male pastor referring to God as "he," the child will come to image God as male.

The Christian church has also used color imagery in noninclusive ways. For instance, consider this well-known passage in Isaiah: "The people who walk in darkness have seen a great light; those who lived in a land of deep darkness on them light have shined." The prophecy is demonstrating that dwelling in the light is better than living in the land of darkness. The imagery of light is used to promote wholeness, revelation, God's intervention. Darkness conjures images of hell, sin, devastation. Inadvertently, we support racism, and racism supports the power of the dominant group because we also refer to the color of a person's skin with words such as "light" or "dark." I may also add that the word "light" should be better translated into "daylight" or "sunlight," and "darkness" as "nightfall."

The liturgical calendar of the Christian church also promotes the use of color imagery. The liturgical color white is used for baptismal outfits, wedding dresses, and other events that symbolize purity and goodness. The liturgical color of black is used for funerals and other solemn occasions. White is the color of the parchments worn as stoles by clergy to signal the major holy seasons in the Christian church: Easter and Christmas.

Our church no longer subscribes to these liturgical colors. We have yet to find a way to respect this tradition and not promote racist imagery of white and black, light and darkness. I found that most people were not even aware of the symbolism of the colors. Therefore, I wear a variety of liturgical colors. Like the paintings of Jesus in the church that portray him as a white American male, there are several indications in a segregated church that intentionally or unintentionally seek to preserve the status quo and thus power.

Summary

To be able to know the fullness of who God is and the way God intervenes in our lives, we must interact with persons from other cultural groupings. If God creates all of us in God's image, then we should image God with an inclusive projection embodying all ethnic and cultural groupings. This also means that I need to learn how to relate to people of different cultural groupings. It is through relationships that I experience God. When I only can see God as a European American male, I see a very narrow perception of who God is. The multicultural church projects an inclusive image of God in its mission to include diverse cultural groupings in its membership.

CHAPTER FOUR

In the Wilderness

Dynamics of Resistance

Several years ago, the Boy Scouts of America made a public proclamation that homosexual males would be excluded from participating in their organization. First Congregational Church of Randolph had a long history of supporting the Boy Scouts, but the last troop had been losing members and eventually folded. A few of the previous leaders were interested in beginning a new troop and approached the church about signing a new charter. I decided that the best approach was to bring the issue before the deacons, especially since several UCC churches in our area had not renewed their present charter or were not signing any new ones.

Three men who had been involved in the Boy Scouts as children and teenagers were a part of the discussion. One of the men had attained his Eagle Scout pin. As we discussed whether we should sign the charter, these men became very defensive of the organization. They witnessed the difference that the Boy Scouts had made in their lives. They argued that just because the administrative policymakers had made this statement against admitting homosexuals, that didn't necessarily reflect the views of its leaders or the scouts themselves. Some wondered whether the boys could be part of scouting as long as they didn't reveal that they were gay. To discern a fuller understanding of the issue, we raised a number of questions. Do we support the Boy Scouts in spite of their decision to bar homosexuals? What will the ramifications be if we supported a troop and a member decided to challenge that policy? Would he have our support against the power of the organization? As we promote inclusiveness, could we support an organization that practices exclusivity? Doesn't that send a contradictory message to the community?

The transitioning from a segregated church to a multicultural church was not an easy journey. It is not my intention to mislead the reader that after we made the decision to become a multicultural church, it was smooth sailing from thereon. Quite the contrary, as members were faced with difficult issues confronting contemporary society, they had new questions that had never before been asked. As the world around us changes, there is a force within the church working to produce a homeostatic balance to make everything stay the same.

In this chapter, I will share our story of resistance. The story contains moments of frustration and discouragement as well as surprising graces that God blessed us with along the way. Just when I thought we had encountered an insurmountable barrier—a great rock in the middle of our path seemed to block us from going any further—God gave us the strength to move it and/or the vision to see our way around it. There were moments when we prayed for bread to fill our spiritual hunger, and God rained manna from heaven. As we confessed that we had worshiped power over worshiping the respect for cultural diversity, we were able to melt the golden calf we had constructed in our midst.

I compare this resistance to the Israelite experience in the wilderness. After being freed from the plagues and liberated from the dominance of the Egyptians, they found themselves in the wilderness of Sinai. When times got tough, they complained to Moses that they were better off in Egypt because at least the land was familiar and they had food to eat. At their moment of desperation, they worried that God had brought them into the wilderness to die. And just when all hope seemed lost, they arrived at the border of the promised land.

If the church were not moving forward, there would be no resistance. Thus, resistance is a sign of hope that the congregation has momentum to move in the direction of the promised land. Multicultural leaders anticipate these dynamics of resistance as people sense this movement and say, "We are really changing." Even though people in the congregation will have moments when they protest these changes, others will respond by recommitting themselves to the journey.

In this chapter, I will examine three dynamics of resistance that we encountered in the wilderness. By identifying these dynamics, leaders will be better equipped to choose a strategy to reduce the risks of sabotage that resistance may cause in the process. If resistance is not dealt with, it has the potential to strengthen its influence and do damage. As long as the congregation shares in the multicultural vision and continues to believe that becoming a multicultural church is what God wants them to do, they will find the strength to rechannel the energy from the wind of resistance towards the promised land.

The Denial of Obstacles

The first dynamic that arose was the denial of obstacles. These obstacles were things about us that were counterproductive to becoming multicultural. Moreover, they were things that we could not easily see. There are aspects about ourselves that we could not see but others could, we needed to ask people for their feedback. Churches are the same way. There are certain qualities about the Christian church that Christians who attend cannot see. One way to deal with this resistance is to go out into the community and ask people about their perceptions of the church.

Over the past fifty years, a large Jewish community had lived in Randolph. There are still several synagogues in the community. Today, however, many of the Jews have moved to a more affluent community, thus making room for those who can afford to move to Randolph from inner-city Boston. African Americans began purchasing these homes about twenty years ago. Interestingly, there are few Hispanic Americans living in Randolph, but there are many who live in a nearby town. As a Spanish speaker, I have performed several weddings and funerals for the Hispanic American community, but they have not yet attended our church.

First Congregational Church of Randolph is directly in the center of town. There are approximately thirty-three thousand residents. The church is a classic New England–style white building which historically has welcomed European American worshipers. It is a long, rectangular structure with a steeple. Its members will smile with pride if you tell them that they have a beautiful sanctuary. Red carpet, plain pews (no pew cushions), and red velvet curtains line the white walls. In the chancel over the communion table hangs a large gold cross. The choir loft is up on the channel. The split chancel consists of the pulpit on one side and the lectern on the other. There is a balcony in the back of the church (from the perspective of the pulpit) that seats about seventy-five people. The sanctuary doesn't get much more traditional looking than that.

Unfortunately, the building and the sanctuary are two of our biggest obstacles to becoming multicultural. Initially, we thought they were assets. The perception is that a "traditional" church holds a "traditional" worship service and clings to traditional thinking. It is difficult to convince the community that we like contemporary worship when the building looks traditional. If it were financially possible for us to make one change, it would be to redesign the building. The chancel is too small for our liturgical dancers, and the praise band is usually quite crowded when it sets up drums and a keyboard. Presently, there is not much we can do about this obstacle. However, we need to pray about it to see if there is a way we can use what we have for our benefit—or at least find a way to go around it.

Another obstacle is our affiliation with the United Church of Christ. Most African Americans in our community attend the Baptist church. Asian Americans are not often Christian. Hispanic Americans are likely to be Catholic or Pentecostal. Almost no persons of color sought out our church because they had a former relationship with another United Church of Christ church. (One woman came because she thought we were affiliated with the Church of Christ.) This presented us with two options: Either we disassociate our relationship with the United Church of Christ or we work towards helping the United Church of Christ become multiracial and multicultural. We felt called to the second option.

Our church responded to the United Church of Christ's "God is Still Speaking" television advertisement campaign during the advent and lenten season of 2004–5. Most people had assumed that all churches in the United Church of Christ were already multicultural. Others could not understand why we would spend money to attract culturally diverse persons if we were already culturally diverse. For this reason, the committee on ministry requires our in-care students to visit other churches. My church denies that we are any different from any other United Church of Christ. As someone nicely summed it up, "We are a traditional, multicultural church."

One other obstacle worth noting is the perception of why people of diverse ethnic groupings come together. One often-held perception by those who live in segregated communities is that people live in multiethnic neighborhoods because they cannot afford to live in a segregated community. The myth is that "it is better to live in a segregated community if one has the money." Another perception is that people move into multiethnic neighborhoods because their own ethnic grouping is represented there, and they want to live with people who share their culture. There is a new generation that is moving into culturally diverse communities because they perceive benefits to living in a multicultural environment.

In communities where white people are still the predominant ethnic grouping, they tend to maintain their power. In Randolph, the politicians are mostly European American, as are the police, fire department, and school officials. An organization called RUN (Randolph Unity Network) is a group of community and religious leaders who confront injustice. The church works with these community groups to advocate for change. A barrier to becoming a multicultural church in a community that is largely European American is that the European American community members will come to expect that its institutions and organizations will subscribe to the dominant-marginalized group structure.

By confronting these barriers and not functioning in a state of denial, we were able to make sound decisions about how to overcome these dynamics and continue forward on the journey.

The Regressive Pull

Social systems are able to manage change as long as they do not experience heightened stress. During stages of change, if an event causes an increased level of stress, there tends to be a pull to regress to old ways of functioning in an attempt to alleviate anxiety. Everyone seems happy with the changes required to become a multicultural church as long as they don't seem to disrupt the church's functioning, i.e., budget, attendance, and/or liturgy. When any of these three areas are affected, there may be signs of discomfort. Moving from segregation to multiculturalism entails afflicting the comfortable. The task of change is to teach people how to manage their discomfort.

There were two incidents of regression that signaled resistance in the church. Like Pharaoh, the dominant group, those who were quite aware that they were called to share their power had second thoughts about changing. It was suggested that in order to bring in new people, we should establish six-week-long membership classes. Attendance to the class would be mandatory for those wishing to join the church. The suggestion was made to change the bylaws to read, "Every person who desires church membership will attend a six-week new membership class." In reality, the class would have been taught by those in the dominant group to share their knowledge of "the way we do things around here."

Some wanted to know what the benefits would be to the church by making it more difficult to join. The dominant group responded that the new-member class was a way for new people to get to know long-term members as well as others new to the church. They would provide child care and make special allowances for those who had to work late or had other scheduling problems. Opponents could not articulate what they did not like about the idea, although a number of people commented that the mentally challenged persons in our membership would not have been able to become members by going through a class. The dominant group picked up quite a few people in the crossfire who thought it was a wonderful idea. It was suggested that the matter come before our annual meeting.

As more and more immigrants enter the United States, there is a tendency to regress to previous policies of curbing immigration to control the influx. There is a direct correlation between the number of immigrants applying for citizenship and the swing of the pendulum between lenient legislation and making it more difficult to enter. We found the same dynamic operative in the church. The more new people came from other cultural groupings, the stricter the church wanted to become about its entrance requirements.

I affectionately refer to the bylaws as the dominant group's weapon of choice. Whenever the dominant group perceives it is losing power, it goes straight for the bylaws as its defense. The problem is that the bylaws were devised by a dominant group whose legacy to the church is sustaining the power of the long-term member. It is this group that most of the bylaws seek to protect, and almost none were designed to protect the welfare of the community at large. Church bylaws are often vague enough to be applicable to any situation that the dominant group can use to further its own agenda.

Jesus preached against adhering to bylaws that go against honoring all persons. He warned against not pulling one's ox out of a hole because it is Sunday. If one is hurt, one should not respond because it is the law. His message was to honor persons above the law and to exclude no one.

The second illustration of the regressive pull involves clapping. It is symbolic of other changes in the worship service, but clapping is the identified problem. I have received more complaints about clapping than Moses received from hungry people starving to death in the wilderness. Basically, the issue goes like this: Some people believe that clapping during the worship service feels like an audience judging a performance. Others use clapping as a response of praise. It relates to their culture and was customary in their previous churches.

The hearing-impaired community rarely clap. The sign for clapping is to raise one's arms in the air and wiggle one's fingers. In a worship service, you will see about half of the people doing this. The other half still claps. There are also people who move to the music;

others are still getting use to that. The regressive pull is to return to a mode of worship by which the worshiper remains still, stoic, and silent.

It became enough of an issue that one Sunday I decided to address both sides during a time in worship we call "The Centering Moment." In order to increase the tolerance of one another, I attempted to help the clappers and nonclappers to see both sides of the issue. Why do we all have to praise God in the same manner? Whenever there is an opportunity to broaden the congregation's perspective, it is a teachable moment. I prefer the hand clap used by the deaf community. I thought I had made a strong argument in favor of hand raising. When I sat down, they all clapped.

The Half-Way Dynamic

The above stories were the most difficult manifestations of resistance that we had encountered. Things were progressing nicely. This wasn't going to be as difficult as we thought. People were observing the changes we were making in moving from a segregated community to a multicultural one. We praised God's creating activity and said, "It is good."

Then on May 17, 2004, Massachusetts passed a law allowing same-gender persons the same legal rights of marriage as heterosexual couples. I had already been performing "unity services" for gays and lesbians, so I saw this change as an opportunity for couples to get health insurance and other rights that historically were only given to heterosexual couples. Before the law passed, I had spoken with several people in the church who anticipated that there could be some resistance to performing a legal ceremony. Much of this resistance was to using the word "marriage" rather than "civil union." We immediately strategized to deal with this resistance. In the worship service, I would read a statement announcing my intentions to marry same-gender persons. So on May 16th, I stood in the center aisle and read the following statement to the congregation:

> Not long ago, it was illegal in Massachusetts for pastors to marry persons of different ethnic backgrounds, and when the law changed, our

church was a forerunner to promote multiculturalism and the equality of all persons. And so when I prayed about the change that will take place tomorrow, I realized that God is calling me, as the pastor of this church, to continue our tradition of being a forerunner, and so I will be marrying same-gender persons in the sanctuary of this church in the same way that I would marry anyone else. And while I realize that there are probably people associated with this church who would not give me their blessing in marrying an interracial couple, I also realize that there may be some who will not give me their blessing to my marrying same-gender persons. I would not let either issue come before a congregational meeting because we're not all going to agree. I thought you should know where I stand and even if you don't agree, I thank you for your continued prayers in my ministry[7].

I sat down and a heavy, tense cloud descended over the congregation. People remained motionless and expressionless. I was afraid that someone might act impulsively. In other words, I was afraid that someone would walk out of the sanctuary. I turned to the man sitting next to me in the choir and motioned for him to look at my hands. They were shaking, and I don't scare easily. The tense situation that I hadn't anticipated raised my anxiety to a fever pitch. I then looked over at the choir sitting across from me and saw one of the elder women trying to get my attention. I was not sure where she stood on the issue. She looked at me and gave me the thumbs-up sign! It was one of those moments of surprising grace.

The conversations that followed went like this: "We've already taken a stand about multiculturalism, which means welcoming all persons. We have supported your ministry of doing unity services, and we even support your marrying same-gender persons–but not in our sanctuary." They got stuck on imagining two persons of the same gender kissing on the chancel. It was too much for some of them to handle. Some suggested that I do the services outside on the front lawn. Others suggested another location altogether. It was a sign of the halfway dynamic. This dynamic occurs when people say, "But we're already welcoming." Do we also have to advocate that diverse cultural groupings all have the same rights? Others felt strongly that gay and lesbian couples should have the right to be married in the church.

I did not discuss the statement with the deacons. I have not yet given enough thought as to whether this was a good idea. Needless to say, they were angry that I did not consult them. But I have turned down couples to be married because I felt they were too young or I suspected abuse. In the past, no one has ever challenged my authority to decide who I will marry and who I will not, so I did not understand why that authority was being challenged now. The good news is that no one was surprised by my statement. As one deacon put it, "How could you have listened to her preach for all these years and not know where she was going to come out on the issue?"

I want to share why I did not allow this issue to be discussed at an annual meeting. We already had several gay and lesbian persons in our midst, some who are "out," and some who are not. I knew that if given the opportunity, prejudice would come forth from people's mouths–somewhat like giving demons a chance to speak. People will say things that they had not really given much thought. However, they would say it as if they had prayed about it and reflected over it for months or even years. In reality, they had not given it much prayerful thought. Prejudice is like toothpaste. Once it's out of the tube, you can't get it back in. I wasn't willing to risk offending those in the gay and lesbian community when it was within my power to prevent it. As Ecclesiastes reminds us, "There is a time to be silent and a time to speak" (3:7).

Two people in the church came to the church council to express their objection. They did not oppose the decision I had made to marry same-gender persons; they opposed that I had made the decision without a congregational meeting. They used the bylaws to demand that the congregation take some action to reprimand me. I defended my position, but after an hour and a long day, I started crying in the meeting. Everyone knows that I cry easily. And even though I am usually quite embarrassed by it, I do it often from the pulpit. I felt worn down. But I realized this could not get better. Inadvertently, or as I usually say, it was "the work of the Holy Spirit," I had given people something to object to. This took the focus away from the issue. They were only objecting that I had not brought the matter to a congregational meeting. Thus, I concluded, they were supporting my decision to marry same-gender persons.

The amount of support I received from people in the congregation was overwhelming. These people concluded that we cannot go halfway through the wilderness and still expect to reach the promised land. The suggestion was made that I would preach a series of sermons on the topic, "What the Bible Says about Homosexuality." I am more than happy to discuss the matter with opponents, but as a Hebrew bible scholar, I am only willing to do that with persons who are fluent in Hebrew. Otherwise, we are only debating the accurateness of our English translations.

I will summarize my response to the more common passages that are selected to defend the position that homosexuality is a sin. But I begin by making the comment that those words do not appear anywhere in Hebrew or Greek. They are a paraphrase of Leviticus 18:22, which states, "You shall not lie with a male as with a woman; it is an abomination." The Hebrew word is *shakab*, which is not the usual word or euphemism for having sex. In Ecclesiastes 4:11, the word is used when two or three people lie down together to keep themselves warm. Leviticus uses different words to connote having sex, which is translated as "to approach" and "to uncover the nakedness of." Whatever the verb means, it is an abomination (*to'evah*), not the word for sin (*hita*). When people say to me, "but the bible says that homosexuality is a sin," I ask them to show me where it says that. They can't because it's not there.

I also want to make a few comments about the often-cited Genesis 19 and Judges 19 stories, which share a parallel thematic structure. Men of the community surround the house of the host and demand that the male visitors be cast out so that the men can rape them. Instead, the host offers the daughters/concubines in their place. These are not stories that are commenting on homosexuality (culturally, we have no idea what the Bible says about the topic because it was probably not something that people talked about). Rather, they are stories about rape, and rape only looks like sex. Rape is about power.

The stories are quite applicable to the multicultural church for another reason. They show what can happen when people hoard power or exercise power for evil purposes over other people. Sex is an act between two consenting adults with an equal distribution of power. To confuse these stories with the act of sex misses the point. God abhors when one group of people dominates another group of people to render them powerless and marginalized. This is a powerful message to the dominant group who is excluding the GLBT community from the Christian church.

People Who Were Resistant

These are observations about our journey. Your journey may be different. But there were three groups of people who manifested the most resistance to my decision to marry same gender persons. By identifying these groups, I hope to equip the reader to see the issue from the perspective of those who had concerns. We know how to effectively strategize when we shift from a narrow to a broad focus.

Gays and lesbians who had yet to come out were the first resistant group. If one devotes most of one's life and psychic energy to hiding something about oneself, then one might resent anyone who begins focusing on what they have spent a lifetime hiding. In our case, the congregation was now paying full attention to the subject. One man shared with me, "I've spent my life in this church trying to get them to look the other way." This group reacted angrily about that which they worked to keep hidden was now out in plain view. If the issue was being talked about in social circles, their fear was that others would be more conscious of the probability that there were gay and lesbian persons in their midst and thus figure it out. They felt a loss of power to continue to conceal it, and they felt that their coming out had been forced upon them.

The second group (and there is no specific order) were African Americans, who were generally respectful of most ethnic groupings. I began by asking them, "Can you help me understand why black people in this church are so upset about my marrying same gender persons?" One African American woman told me, "I resent that they claim the same experience of oppression. Their experience is much different from ours. Our people were sold into slavery. They were raped, and murdered, chained, and were victims of horrible injustices. We were taken from our home and brought to this land. Gay and lesbian people just wake up one day and decide to become homosexual. They have it easy."

A Haitian American man answered this way: "When I walk into a room, everyone knows I'm black. I can't hide it like gay and lesbian people. They don't experience the same prejudice we do because our 'otherness' is on our skin. Therefore, if they can hide it, they can choose which situations they will be marginalized and which situations they can be part of the dominant group. I don't get that choice."

The third group didn't fit into one specific cultural grouping. Some were parents of gay and lesbian children who were resistant for the same reasons that their children expressed. Some were already angry with me, and any controversial issue that arose was reason enough to join in the resistance against the pastor. One woman resigned her membership from the church. I sent her a nice note saying that I was sorry we did not agree on this issue, and I wished her well.

Other Arguments

Objections ran the gamut of people's irrational thinking. Some asked if I would be willing to marry a man and his daughter or a woman and her dog. I politely told them that both of those arrangements are illegal in Massachusetts and that my intention was merely to uphold the law. I was not making a statement about whether I promote homosexuality as an alternative or a mainstream lifestyle, but I was making a statement about obeying the law as a citizen of the commonwealth.

I also stated that I am not in favor of civil ceremonies as a way to consecrate the relationship between two people. When a couple goes to the justice of the peace to be married, they do not receive premarital counseling. One of the major reasons that people seek out a pastor to perform a wedding is for the opportunity to discuss personal issues that might be affecting their relationship. Premarital counseling is not only to discuss the seventeen-minute wedding service. If we encourage people to be married outside of the church, they may be ill prepared for the marriage after the wedding. I believe that marriage is a sacred covenant performed in the eyes of God.

Therefore, my stance is that I will marry anyone whom Massachusetts law states can be married and can produce a marriage license for me to sign. That doesn't mean that I will perform the ceremony. (If I suspect there has been abuse, I will often refer for counseling.) But every couple who can be married should be married in a sanctuary by a pastor rather than by a justice of the peace on a beach. It is not within the realm of my authority who the law determines can be married, but it is within my authority to determine where they will be married. I asked people, "Wouldn't you expect your pastor to take the position that all people should be married in the sanctuary?" Most people eventually agreed.

And the Story Continues

After the momentum was moving again, it was suggested that we place an ad in a major newspaper in the Boston area. It read:

> *The First Congregational Church of Randolph* invites *all* couples to be married in its sanctuary. *For an appt. call (church phone number)*

The deacons were in favor of placing the ad. They knew it would stir up controversy but felt it was time to make a statement to the community. Then we had to discuss where we would get the money to pay for the ad. The man who had been an Eagle Scout and had voiced strong opposition against our not supporting the Boy Scouts' stance on homosexuality offered to pay for the ad. It was one of those surprising graces when we could witness to the progress of our multicultural movement and the dance of the Holy Spirit. It was also a testimony about my ministry at the church. People were listening.

Since the ad appeared in the paper, we have had an increase in gay and lesbian persons worshiping with us on Sunday morning. It was our way of announcing to the community where we stood on the issue. There were still people who felt we had gone too far in placing the ad. "Do we really need to announce it to everyone?" The answer is yes.

The surprising grace was that people who had been among the voices of opposition were transformed by the spirit and became some of our best evangelists for the multicultural movement. They understood where people were coming from who were resistant to the changes and could address their concerns. They could say, "I used to think that, too, but now I see the issue from another perspective." As they witnessed to their own transformation, they convinced others to be open to the power of the Holy Spirit to transform them, too.

CHAPTER FIVE

Revelation at Mt. Sinai

Ten Commandments for the Multicultural Church

IN HIS BOOK *The Wolf Shall Dwell with the Lamb,* Eric Law warns that when culturally diverse persons come together, there is potential for misunderstanding and conflict. "When a wolf is together with other wolves, everything is fine. When a lamb is together with other lambs, everything is safe and sound. But if you put a wolf and a lamb together, inevitably something bad is going to happen. Some people are so disheartened by it that they are giving up the idea of integration altogether."[1] The wolf wants to invite the lamb to play a game, but the wolf insists that the lamb play by its rules. The lamb is not sure how to play the game. The wolf assumes the lamb should know how to play because "every animal knows how to play this way," even though the rules were devised by the wolf community. The lamb remembers the last time someone in his family played with a wolf; they were devoured by the wolf.

When Moses brought the children of Israel into the wilderness, problems arose. So God called the leader of the movement to the top of the mountain to dispense the rules for interaction–the Ten Commandments. Social groups are formed with a set of rules to encourage conformity. By outlining normative, acceptable behavior, the risk of acting out is reduced. These rules determine the boundary line between behavior that is allowed and behavior that is not. Before the wolf and the lamb are invited to play a game together, they should both participle in designing and agree with the rules.

When we began the journey toward multiculturalism, I confess I thought that it was only a matter of inviting racially and ethnically diverse people to worship in our church. I anticipated that if people had the opportunity to interact by serving on committees and eating together, they would get along fine. On one occasion, I was confused as to why a person of color stormed out of a committee meeting one night. I wondered why all the African Americans sat in the back of the church or in the balcony. We had brought together culturally diverse people who had different perceptions of "the way things should be," and sometimes those ways were in direct conflict with one another. And the more comfortable the wolf and the lamb came to be in a multicultural environment; the more they voiced those different perspectives.

Historical Patterns of Interaction

Perhaps the most serious mistake we made was disrespecting the histories of marginalized groups and their historical experiences of interfacing with European Americans. Stories such as *To Kill a Mockingbird* remind us of the violence that has been perpetrated by white people against black people. European Americans do not want to relive that history because it makes us feel guilty. Oftentimes we use the defense, "but it wasn't me." We desire only to move forward and want to disconnect ourselves from our historical pattern of interacting with black people. We want black people to do the same. In the eyes of many people of color, the white community has not confessed the sins of their fathers. We cannot ask for forgiveness until we admit that we have sinned.

> When African Americans emphasize their right to defend themselves against those who seek to destroy their community, it never fails that so-called white Christians then ask, "What about the biblical doctrine of reconciliation?" "What about Christian forgiveness?" "Can't black people find it in their hearts to forgive us?" Those who are responsible for the dividing walls of hostility, racism, and hatred want to know whether the victims are ready to forgive and forget without changing the balance of power.[2]

European Americans detach from that aspect of our ancestors in order to protect ourselves from feeling guilty. But the lamb knows that "the apple doesn't fall far from the tree." Today, it is true that it is less acceptable to be violent toward the other; perhaps our weapons of violence have only become more discreet, not less destructive. People of color are still passed over for promotions or are hired because the employer has to fill affirmative-action policies. Gays and lesbians are denied the same civil rights as heterosexual persons. Many public places are not handicap accessible, or are so limited in terms of accessibility, that it becomes a hassle for a disabled person to navigate entrance into a building or use some mode of transportation.

Eric Law observes that in some situations, when black and white people interact, white people take charge and black people let them. This is one of the most prevalent historical patterns of interaction. Some white people may want to befriend black people; however, they want to relate to black people in the same way that their ancestors related to them: by asserting power over them. This is the way that the game is played. White people seem to be unaware of this, but just because we are unaware, it doesn't mean that it isn't still operative. We are still responsible for our sins, even if we are ignorant to our actions. "I didn't mean to do it" is not a defense if someone has pointed it out to us and we continue to repeat the same pattern of behavior. White people are so used to being in charge that they assume it is in everyone's best interests and that everyone wants to play the game this way.

I recently heard about a white church that had decided to form a partnership with an inner-city black church. The white church invited the black church to participate in a fellowship dinner at their church. When the members of the black church showed up, members of the white church didn't want to be rude (by white standards), so they invited their guests to have a seat (they all sat together) and served them a meal (and didn't invite their guests to help prepare it). Afterward, to avoid any awkwardness between the groups, the white members orchestrated an array of entertainment. The white church thought the experience was "wonderful." But when they contacted the black church about doing it again, the black church politely declined.

In this chapter, I set forth a ten commandments, or "rules for interaction" for the multicultural church. The Christian church talks a lot about peace, justice, and reconciliation, but there has to be some practicality to those terms to make them relevant. In other words, how do we enact peace? What does justice look like in the congregational life of the Christian church? How do we know when we have achieved reconciliation?

The Purpose of These Ten Commandments

Jesus is asked, "Teacher, which commandment in the law is the greatest?" He replied, "You shall love the Lord your God with all your heart, and with all your soul and with all your mind. This is the greatest and first commandment. And a second is like it: 'You shall love your neighbor as yourself'" (Matthew 22:36–39). Above all the other commandments the commandment to love God is first lifted by Jesus, followed by our neighbor as ourselves. The question for us is to define love and discern what love looks like in a multicultural environment.

Faith communities should be places where everyone loves each other and gets along. In actuality, churches are breeding grounds for dysfunctional behavior. What people would not be allowed to do in other social systems, they easily get away with it in the Christian church. I have witnessed people being mean, stealing power from others, and letting evil dominate their lives. Contrary to popular opinion, Christians are not on their best behavior when in God's house. People with patterns of dysfunctional behavior cannot turn off those patterns in a church community. They bring their dysfunctional patterns with them. Unlike other institutions, however, the church is in a position to confront dysfunctional and hurtful behavior in a loving, caring manner.

A multicultural church constructs a process of accountability for those who transgress the commandments. There is no dominant group that oversees this process and enables individuals to be passive bystanders when prejudice is practiced. People will not learn how to get along if they run to a third party to resolve their disputes. For learning to take place from church to community, parishioners need to feel empowered to hold each other accountable. Such an expectation puts pressure on those to conform to the rules and to change their dysfunctional behavior—which, in some cases, might need to be reinforced with therapy. Unlike a segregated church that is experiencing the plague of declining numbers and says, "We can't afford to lose anybody," the multicultural church might find itself in a position to exclude the person who does not conform. This practice of exclusion is not based on cultural grouping but on cultural sensitivity.

Commandment 1: Thou Shall Not Deny Difference[3]

During one Lent, I was invited to preach at a neighboring church. An elderly woman came through the line to shake my hand and said, "You were so good; for a moment, I forgot you were a woman." Was she implying that when God created me, God made a mistake? What are the ramifications for denying our difference in the Christian church?

I recently had a conversation with a seminarian who shared with me that her denomination will ordain her as long as she does not claim in writing that she is a lesbian. I shared with her that I had concerns about her participating as a leader in a system that promotes the denial of difference. How does that denial translate to those whose difference is genetic, biological, or physical and does not lend itself to being hidden? When we ask leaders of the church to hide their differences, what message are we sending to the wider community about the acceptability of difference? How can we have the conversation about multiculturalism if the Christian church seeks to deny there is multiness in its midst?

I also responded to her as a heterosexual parishioner. Each Sunday, if I listen intently to the pastor's sermon and trust her word, and then one Sunday she reveals (or I figure out) that she is a lesbian, I might feel betrayed and wonder, "What else has she been hiding?" I might be aware of the denominational policy that mandated she hide this part of herself from the congregation, but that also may reduce my allegiance to that denomination. I might be most concerned that she did not trust that this particular faith community would be supportive, and so I might be suspicious of those around me.

One ramification of this hiding pattern of interaction is that it contributes to a parishioner's lack of comfort when it comes to sharing their faith. Most churches attempt to provide opportunities for sharing—through Bible study, workshops, etc.—in an atmosphere where trust is developed and nurtured. The church should be a place for this level of sharing, especially when there are few other social systems that provide such an opportunity. If the church becomes one more institution where people have their defenses in place, they will treat their relationship with the church in the same manner as they treat their relationship with others institutions. Encouraging people to deny their difference is counterproductive to building a community where one feels comfortable in sharing one's faith.

Commandment 2: Thou Shall Not Categorize by Cultural Grouping

One of our ministers, ordained in the African Methodist Episcopal church and seeking privilege of call with the United Church of Christ, was working on a paper for his UCC polity class. As he sat in my office at my computer, he began making a list of the worship leaders. He said, "Let's see, we have two African American pastors, a German American pastor, and a Chinese American pastor." He paused. There was one pastor left, an openly lesbian woman, and I assumed he was trying to find the words to indicate her sexual orientation. Finally, he looked at me and said, "I think she is Italian American." I had never thought about her ethnic grouping. I only saw her as a lesbian. He taught me something about my tendency to categorize people by their cultural grouping.

Somewhat on the other end of the continuum of acknowledging our differences is the tendency to see only our differences, or to see specific differences. If we only see people in terms of their sexual orientation, we will be unable to appreciate the traditions that are important to their ethnic background. I am more than a heterosexual, middle-class, European American woman. I am also a quilter, a Boston marathoner, and a liturgical dance teacher. I am a wife, a mother, and a friend. I am more than the sum of my cultural groupings.

When we meet someone for the first time, we tend to categorize them by racial groupings, e.g,. "the black man who was sitting in the front pew last Sunday." What we notice about another person is their birth and physical characteristics, and these observations provide us with a link to others we have known with similar traits. We assess how to interact with that person based on categories of racial and cultural groupings. In other words, we act differently to someone who has power over us.

This tendency crosses the line into prejudice when we assume that we know certain qualities about a person based on the categorizing of racial and cultural groupings. People assume that all African Americans want to hear gospel music in the worship service. Adults assume that all teenagers like the music of the late rapper Tupac. The music committee worried that the elder persons in our church would object to replacing the beloved Pilgrim Hymnal with a new one. Interestingly, we found that some black people wanted to hear anything but gospel music because they were looking for something new and different. Some of the teenagers expressed disappointment to find that our new hymnal doesn't have "Lord, I Want to be a Christian" in it. We have learned not to assume that one's racial and cultural grouping is a predictor or indicator of one's likes and dislikes.

Commandment 3: Thou Shall Not Practice Ethnocentrism

> Many people have observed, for example, that American churches that mix blacks and whites in their membership can do reasonably well as long as the blacks remain a numerical minority. In such cases, the burden for altering the system of relevance has fallen on the black membership. This relationship is acceptable particularly to those blacks who have assimilated into the Anglo-American culture or who

are moving in that direction. The whites are glad to have them as long as they "do it our way."[4]

Ethnocentrism holds to the belief that there is a right way to do things that are ethnic-specific. Some European Americans believe that the right way is the "white way." In other words, any other way is the wrong way. Thus, the dominant group sustains its power because of a belief that it holds the knowledge to differentiate between right and wrong and convinces others that it has access to this knowledge while others do not. The marginalized group is then dependent upon the dominant group to share its knowledge and accept it as gospel. Tony Matthews identifies "ecclesiastical ethnocentrism" as one of the major barriers to becoming a multicultural church.[5]

In a segregated European American church, the perception is that there is a right way to enter God's house. One comes in, shakes the hand of a greeter (often someone in power), and sits in one's designated space. If one sits in a different pew, one might upset the homeostatic balance, and the church might tip over. God forbid that a visitor disrupts the right way by attempting to sit in someone else's pew. Even the way we greet visitors connotes power. Visitors receive a bulletin so they can follow along with the way we do things. They are then escorted to a pew where they are allowed to sit. For one who has experienced marginality from the Christian church, the very act of entering the church can be a confrontation with one's marginal status.

In a segregated European American church, the perception is that there is also a right way to conduct oneself during the worship service. One is suppose to be silent, still, and expressionless. I refer to this pattern of interaction as "the oil-painting effect." From the viewpoint of the worship leaders, it is like we are standing before an oil painting at an art gallery. No one moves. I remember the first time I spontaneously said something funny. People looked around at each other trying not to laugh and trying to discern whether it was acceptable to do so in a worship service. At the current time, clapping has become the focus of disagreement. Some see it as disrespectful, reinforcing the concept of "performance with an audience." Others see it as a way to praise God. The debate continues.

The important matter to note is that the church has moved beyond the perception that their way is the only way. They now recognize that there are differences in the way that people worship; sometimes based on likes and dislikes and past experiences, sometimes based on the traditions of one's cultural grouping.

Law states,

> The first step toward becoming a multicultural community is to recognize our own tower of Babel–our ethnocentrism. Each cultural grouping has a tendency to make itself superior, believing that its tower is better and taller and can reach the heavens. In a multicultural community, we need to identify our tower of Babel and decide to consciously stop building it. We need to come down from our tower and see others on level ground. . . . As we climb down from our tower, we examine each brick and wall, learning how we got that high. When we finally land-with a fuller consciousness and acceptance of who we are— we are ready to encounter others who have also come down from their towers.

Commandment 4: Thou Shall Resolve Conflict by Maintaining Honor

According to Duane Elmer, "In a shame culture, the worst thing one person can do is to cause another to be shamed, lose face, or be dishonored. . . . It is considered an even greater tragedy if this shaming is done in public. To be shamed or lose face before one's family, friends or esteemed colleagues is to be avoided at all costs."[6] Elmer suggests that there are two strategies to resolve conflict and maintain honor. First, leaders can find a mediator between the parties whose neutrality does not threaten the power of either party. The second strategy is for party A to explain to party B the potential risk that party A might be dishonored and to invoke the help of party B to preserve its honor. When one is asked for assistance to sustain honor, most people will do whatever lies in the realm of their power. We are honored by the very act of being asked for help. The person asking for help is communicating to us that they perceive that we are able to help them.

Commandment 5: Thou Shall Practice Empathy

Empathy is the ability to image oneself in the body of another, and to imagine what they must be feeling so that words of encouragement can be offered. It is not just a matter of walking in someone else's shoes; it is a process whereby our perspective—and henceforth the way we relate—is changed.

Job's friends tried to comfort Job in his moment of despair. Instead of attempting to understand what it must have been like for Job to lose his family, his health, and his possessions, they created distance between themselves and Job. By assuming that he must have done something to bring on the wrath of God, Job's friends believed that God was punishing him. Therefore, they were able to distance themselves rather than provide empathy. They distanced themselves by thinking, "That couldn't happen to me because whatever he did to bring that on himself, I would never do." Had they entertained the idea that it could have happened to anyone, including themselves, they might have had some empathy for Job and helped him in his situation.

Becoming a multicultural church depends on people who can imagine what it is like to be marginalized. By developing this insight, those in a multicultural church enter into another person's world and see it from their perspective. Situations are viewed differently when we gain a different perspective. In the process, we become less judgmental and more tolerant. We need to connect with experiences in our own lives that may have caused us to feel rejected, powerless, and excluded in order to be able to connect to the experience of others. By getting in touch with those feelings and experiences, we may be better equipped to make decisions regarding the way we interact with others.

Commandment 6: Thou Shall Ask Questions

If my grandmother died and you came to comfort me, you might show empathy by saying, "My grandmother died, too." I might feel some connection with you because you have had a similar experience. But my experience might be quite different depending on a number of factors, some related to my cultural grouping, some not. You might say to me, "I imagine you must feel very sad about losing your grandmother." You are attempting to offer empathy by connecting with how you felt when your grandmother died. But the death of my grandmother might be cause for celebration because she left me a million dollars in her will. Perhaps my grandmother was a nasty, bitter woman whose death signals a new age for our family's mental health. Your experience might not be my experience, and you may need to ask me questions about mine.

I can tell you what it is like for me to enter a room full of male colleagues and have no one acknowledge my presence. I know what it is like to have my profile placed in the trash because people are saying, "Laurene Bowers, that sounds like a woman!" I have my own experience of marginality, but I cannot assume that your experience is the same as mine. Instead, I need to ask you questions such as, "What is it like when the color of your skin prevents you from getting a job?" or "What is it like not to be allowed to join a local country club because of your religion?" I am communicating, "Help me to understand what it is like to be you." If you are genuinely interested in my experience in order to connect with me as a Christian, then I am willing to share with you what it's like to be me.

It is often said that "everyone has a story that would break your heart." The multicultural church operates with this perspective. If I cannot imagine what it is like to be in a situation that you are experiencing, I need to ask questions to understand your perspective. We tend to worry that if we ask questions, we are being nosy, but asking questions shows interest in the person's situation. If people perceive that the other has genuine interest, most people will talk about themselves, their life experiences, and their relationship with God. As a pastor, my experience has taught me that most people are desperately seeking these opportunities, especially within the church.

Commandment 7: Thou Shall Foremost Preserve the Relationship

Elmer observes that in two thirds of the world, one may agree with others, especially those with power, in order to preserve the relationship. He refers to this dynamic as "the relational yes." People will say "Yes" when they really mean "No" because they do not want to lose face or experience shame. The problem often surfaces when the dominant group rejoices because "everyone is in favor of it," when in reality only those of the dominant group really favor it. In congregational meetings, this dynamic happens frequently. The marginalized group sums up the direction in which the dominant group is moving. They then show support for that direction–but can be swayed if the decision goes the other way.

While this is an example of what historically happens when dominant and marginalized groups come in contact; it calls us to pay attention to the importance of relationships. European Americans tend to want to be right rather than preserve relationships. They need to prove their point in order to convince others that they are right and others are wrong. They are less concerned with whether this threatens the relationship. A person of color may say, "Okay, I agree with you," when they want to align themselves with white power to protect the relationship.

Commandment 8: Thou Shall Practice "Gracism"

David Anderson has coined the word "gracism" to encourage people to be more than tolerant of cultural groupings different from one's own. He writes,

> Distinct from favoritism, whereby one grants favor because of elitism, ethnic superiority or commonality, gracism reaches outside these boxes. A gracist reaches across ethnic lines and across racial borders to lend specific assistance and extra grace to those who are different, on the fringe, marginalized . . . . Gracism focuses on race for purposes of ministry and service. When the grace of God is communicated through the beauty of race, then you have gracism.[7]

Gracism sighs when people say, "I would treat him like I treat everybody else," instead of "I am going to go one better and give her the benefit of the doubt." It provides a margin for misunderstanding. When conflict arises and I begin to sense that there is a problem, I first assume that it is my own misperception of the situation, and that if I look at it from a different perspective, I will be able to see that misperception (rather than assume that the other is intentionally trying to pull one over on me). I search for teachable moments when I can suppress my need to assume that the other is being rude, disrespectful, or mean. There is a teachable moment when I attempt to better understand who I am by the way I am likely to respond. Gracism allows people to practice patience with those who might attend a multicultural church but may be mistrustful about the church's intention.

Commandment 9: Thou Shall Not Judge Others

Jesus said, "Do not judge, and you will not be judged" (Luke 6:37).

The protestors have increased their protests since Massachusetts passed the law allowing same gender persons to be married. They hold up signs in public places and recently have showed up at elementary schools. They strongly believe that they are able to judge another because they are in the right. Their mission is to convince others that they, too, have the authority to judge, even though Jesus clearly calls us not to judge others.

As a heterosexual person, my perspective on homosexuality is simply, "I don't get it." But I don't have to "get it" to know that I am called to treat others in Christian love and fight against the evil of hate. It seems that people who judge others are playing God because ultimately we all will be judged before God. When that happens, I go with a clear conscience, knowing that while others might disagree with my perspective, I did not judge anyone but tried to understand the viewpoint of the other.

Commandment 10: Thou Shall Not Hoard Power

In chapter six, I will speak more about the issue of power. For the present moment, I will name it as a pattern of interaction to be resisted in the multicultural church. Here, I will introduce and reiterate some of the key concepts.

- European Americans need to make sure that when they gather with persons of color they do not assert power over them.

- European Americans cannot assume that they own the church because the history of the church is predominantly European American.

- In a multicultural church, the dominant group is convinced to share its power with the marginalized group. Everyone benefits from this redistribution of power.

- Power is assigned based on tasks and functions and is sustained based on performance.

Strategies to Enforce the Commandments: Confrontation with Care

As a microcosm of society, the church will embody persons who will practice prejudice, either overtly through exclusion and or through more subtle means, i.e., tolerance. We can no more exclude persons of prejudice than we can exclude persons from marginalized cultural groupings. The mission of the multicultural church is actually to encourage persons filled with prejudice to come into our midst in order to exorcise their prejudice from them. Through interacting with others and practicing the ten rules for engagement, people learn more appropriate patterns of relating.

When prejudice occurs, those in the room are responsible to confront with care what was said or done. Those who witness the prejudice are also practicing how to confront prejudice when it occurs in the community. Some people perceive that they can be prejudiced if no one stops them. When people of faith do nothing to bring it to their attention, they assume that everyone in the room is in support of their prejudiced perspective. This strengthens their view that they are correct in being prejudiced against another.

Every situation calls for an assessment of the most effective and compassionate strategy. Sometimes it is appropriate to confront others, especially if it can be done in such a way that the person filled with prejudice can maintain their honor. If the potential exists for them to feel shamed, the confrontation should be done in another room or at another time. It is important not to wait too long to confront such a person because people tend to forget what they said. In a Christian community, we say things to people in love and kindness that we might not feel comfortable saying in another setting. This is a manifestation of Christian love.

Summary

These Ten Commandments teach people appropriate patterns of relating to other cultural groupings. The church provides an opportunity for people to practice these patterns, and if they continue to manifest prejudice or regress into old patterns, their brothers and sisters in Christ are responsible to confront them in a caring and loving way.

Chapter Six

Melting the Golden Calf

The Redistribution of Power

ONE NIGHT DURING A COMMITTEE MEETING, we were trying to arrive at a decision on behalf of the congregation. The chairperson asked members if they had a sense of the majority opinion within the congregation. It seemed that we were reaching a consensus—that is, until one member interjected, "But what about Harry? What would Harry say about this?" The conversation came to a screeching halt. With stunned looks, each committee member began to scan the eyes of every other committee member. Trying to keep my composure, I asked, "And why would we be concerned about what Harry thinks? Harry is dead!" A long-term, beloved church member who had served on every committee and in every leadership position, Harry had managed to retain his power even beyond the grave.

What distinguishes a segregated, traditional church from a multicultural one is the way in which power is distributed among its members. In segregated churches, the power base is centralized; that is, approximately fifteen people amass most of the power and run the church. Pastors make decisions by consulting these fifteen people, and it is often irrelevant whether or not they currently serve on a committee or in a leadership position. They retain their power even when not functioning in these roles. If they remain in the group for a significant length of time, they become respected as beloved church members. What they think matters because everyone knows that they can easily influence or sway a decision with their power. Like rooting for our favorite football team, we like to be on the side of the winners. We therefore support those who tend to win an argument or debate in the church because of their power to influence. These fifteen people are the dominant group in the church.

The marginalized group includes everyone else in the congregation. They may enable the dominant group to retain their power because the dominant group has convinced them that they have everyone's best interests at heart. Because the dominant group tends to overfunction and serve the church in a number of different roles, the marginalized group may be relieved that they don't have to participate, only simply come and worship. Those in the marginalized group might say, "He is such a good church member because he does so much for our church." Overfunctioning is equated with being a good church member. Both groups may have an investment in maintaining the status quo.

A problem arises when those in the marginalized group resents that the dominant group has the power, wanting instead to participate and share in that power. When the dominant group hoards power, the marginalized group then has to rationalize why they are not allowed to participate in this inner circle. When the nominating committee seems to be asking the same people to participate over and over again, the marginalized group is confronted with its marginalized status. For ethnic groupings in the church that are in the minority, this experience may conjure up feelings of injustice that they have experienced in other social systems. "As marginality is relative to centrality, everyone tends to seek his or her center is at the center of the dominant group. So ethnic minorities as marginalized people also want to be at the center, even if not as part of the group that claims to be central. Yet the more the minority group seeks to be part of the majority group at the center, the more they feel marginalized."[1] It may reassure the marginalized group to say, "I don't want to play," than to admit that one wants to play but has not been invited.

Everyone, then, appears to be invested in sustaining the power of the dominant group, until a point of crisis. In chapter one, I described the crisis that arose at First Congregational Church. There has to be a point at which the church encounters two paths:

the current path, which is no longer accessible through the woods, or a new path, which is unfamiliar and frightening. Many people feared that becoming a multicultural church would transform it into a faith community in which they did not feel comfortable, or one where the worship service would not meet their spiritual needs. People seem to have a natural tendency to cling blindly to the familiar, even if that path is causing them pain or dysfunction. The church has to be willing to take a leap of faith to tread a new path, one that will lead them out of the wilderness.

Eric Law states that in order to take this new path, the church must shift its power from the dominant group to the marginalized one.

> Together with my colleagues and the people of this community, we created a crossing—the true encounter beyond the ascribed and assumed roles. The way we created this crossing was to facilitate a power shift. Instead of continuing the pattern of a few persons dominating while the majority let them, we created a "grace margin" in which everyone's input was welcome and listened to, where everyone participated. In the process, the seemingly powerful became silent. The seemingly powerless were empowered to speak and they took the lead in the future direction of the church community. In the switching of power, the presence of Christ was made known. We experienced the Word at the Crossing.[2]

I agree with Eric that the dominant group needs to release some of its power in order to empower the marginalized group to participate in decision making, but he seems to suggest that we take power away from the dominant group in order to empower the marginalized. Rather, I will suggest that, ideally, we hope that the dominant group will see that it is in their best interests to share their power with the marginalized group and thus redistribute power based on criteria other than length of membership or willingness to perform a role that no one else in the church wants to do. Power should be distributed based on role. Those who are competent to fulfill a role should have the power to carry out the functions attached to that role. In the church, we assess competence in terms of "gifts."

In this chapter, I will describe the dynamics of power in segregated churches and demonstrate why it is in everyone's best interests to redistribute power. I will offer strategies about how to convince both the dominant group to let go of their hoarded power and the marginalized group, if willing, to accept that power. My central argument is that a multicultural church assigns power based on how much one needs in order to function in a specific role in the life of the congregation. I will also examine the pastor's role as a distributor of power because I believe his or her role is crucial to this shift from the dominant group to the marginalized one.

Power in Segregated Churches

There is no other social institution that distributes power the way the church does. A visitor can attend one week, volunteer for a task that others would shy away from—e.g., lead the youth groups—and be handed unlimited power the following week. Given the plague of declining membership, a visitor who is willing to help out with unpleasant tasks might be such a welcome relief that he or she is given whatever is desired in return. Because the harvest is plentiful but the laborers are becoming scarce, the church is the one institution where those who feel powerless in other areas of life can attend and receive power—that is, they do not have to demonstrate their ability to perform a task well. For instance, they might not have a gift to work with teenagers but volunteer to be the junior high youth leader. Everyone else is relieved that finally someone volunteered to do this task, and so they may bestow power upon this person in exchange for his or her participation.

This leadership position may quickly align this person with other church leaders. If you want to know if a newcomer has an agenda of attaining power, note who they talk with during coffee hour. Those who come to a church looking for power (whether they are conscious of it or not) have an uncanny ability to scope the Fellowship Hall and, with radar, seek out a member of the dominant group. They befriend those in the dominant group because those who are friends with people in power share in that power. When newcomers seem to be looking for a way in, they may be willing to do just about any task if there is some hope of attaining power.

In segregated churches, power is exchanged for level of participation. The more a parishioner engages in a task, the more power he or she accumulates. Not every parishioner who participates has a need for power, and some will be able to manage their power well. Some parishioners will serve as models for others because they only accept the degree of power necessary to accomplish a task; upon completion, they will return that power to the system. When a parishioner retains power even after the task is completed, yet someone new is doing the task, then that parishioner is hoarding power and, in turn, taking that power away from the other person. When hoarding power is allowed in the church, it becomes a lifetime warranty that can be exercised at any future date when the parishioner wants to get his or her way.

It has been my experience that parishioners who hoard power or who come looking to church for power are attempting to counterbalance feelings of powerlessness in other aspects of life. This parishioner may be starved for love, affection, and affirmation. For instance, a parishioner who is being battered by a spouse at home and feels helpless to make it stop might come to church to try to feel some power. This power is not used to empower him or her to get out of the relationship, as the way of functioning in both settings involves someone with power and someone without it. It is important for multicultural leaders to have some sensitivity to why people hoard power. Until we understand why they do this as well as the dynamics that lie below the surface of their motivation, we will not be able to help them to let go of their power.

Why Centralized Power Does Not Work for Multicultural Churches

When we first embarked on the journey to become multicultural, we assumed that other ethnic groups would assimilate into the life of the church, which at the time functioned as "the European American Protestant way." We would not have been able to articulate what that way was exactly, assuming that every church functioned the way we do. In our minds, there was the right way to do things, which we equated with "the white way." This is how "the right way" works: One attends a church, sits in the pew of one's choice, and when asked to serve on a committee, replies, "I will think about it," then thank the person for asking. If one is agreeable to taking on a task, there is an underlying expectation that one will complete it in the same manner as it has been done for the last fifty years. No one is asking you to be creative and let the holy spirit dance within you. The way it has always been done is "the right way." In other words, the white way is not only the right way, but viewed as the only way.

What we came to understand is that diverse ethnic and cultural groupings handle power in different ways. As persons from other cultural groupings began getting involved in the church, we realized that there was a different way of doing things. Initially, we compared the white way to the ways of other ethnic groupings and rushed to our own defense that we were doing it the right way. This meant, however, that other ethnic groupings were doing it "the wrong way."

The crisis point came when we were able to attract diverse ethnic groupings, but they appeared resistant to wanting to do things "our" way. They would agree to serve on committees, but then they would either not show up for the meetings or they would not carry out the tasks assigned to them (often by people in the dominant group). The dominant group took note of this seeming lack of involvement and began to complain. They voiced their perception that "the white people still have to do everything." The second part of that phrase was not articulated but could be filled in as "the other ethnic groupings aren't pulling their weight." The dominant group perceived that the marginalized group didn't want to play, when in reality they did not know the rules of the game.

Whereas we had operated under a committee model where people were nominated and then given tasks, we realized that other ethnic groupings tend to prefer being asked to do a specific task—e.g., to help out in the soup kitchen—rather than serve on the mission committee. We also learned that in a large church, there is a perception that there is no room at the inn. When every committee appears to be full, and committees are the seat of power in which one can participate in the life of the church, then there may appear to be no current vacancies for participating in doing the work of Christ. When one feels like an outsider, one might not come forward to volunteer for fear there may be a person from the dominant group who is also contemplating volunteering. Those in the marginalized group have to worry about stepping on the toes of whoever did the task before, therefore being concerned about the repercussions of coming across as if trying to take that leadership position away from someone who has historically held it.

Congregations that function with centralized power tend to have the same people doing the same tasks and fulfilling the same leadership positions year after year. They may do these functions quite well, so there seems to be no reason to ask anyone else to do them. The problem is that they tend to become possessive of their role and/or their relationship to the wider church. Those who hoard power in the dominant group may perceive that they own the church. It is the same imprint in the European American mind that they own the land of America and all other ethnic groupings are immigrants. I cringe every time I hear someone in the church use the argument, "But this is my church!" I have to remind them that the church belongs to Jesus. We are merely the stewards.

Jesus told a parable about those who show up at different times of the day to serve God (Matt. 20:1–16). A landowner woke up early and went out to hire laborers to work in his vineyard. He went out at 9 AM, noon, 3 PM, and 5 PM. When evening came, the owner of the vineyard said to his manager, "Call the laborers and give them their pay, beginning with the last and then going to the first." When those hired at five o'clock came, they received the usual daily wage. But when the first group came, they expected a greater wage but instead received the agreed-upon amount. Seeing that those hired later received the same wage, they went grumbling to the landowner. Jesus concludes, "So the last will be first and the first will be last" (v.6). The message is clear: length of membership and service in the body of Christ does not entitle the dominant group to more power than the marginalized group.

Making the Shift to Decentralized Power

Everyone loved the director of our Christian Education program. She had been in that job forever. All the kids knew and loved her and grew up in Sunday school under her wisdom and guidance. She was not a particularly good administrator, often forgetting about meetings and ordering the wrong curriculum, but the teachers felt supported by her. Her faith in Jesus shined forth in whatever she said or did, but programs were poorly organized, and people would complain to the pastor that nothing was getting accomplished under her leadership. Is the objective to take away her job and give it to someone more competent? What about relationship-building tasks? Aren't the gifts of communicating faith more important than accomplishing tasks?

A fear arose among the dominant group that if the marginalized group is given power, they will take it and hoard it in the same way that they, the dominant group, hoarded it. In the mighty fortress of hoarded power, there is a fear that if the gate is opened and others are granted access to the realm of power, the marginalized group will push it wide open with such force that the dominant group will get kicked out and become powerless. The fear was that we would not change the way we distributed power but merely substitute one group of people for another: The marginalized would become dominant and vice versa. It was the "vice versa" that worried the dominant group.

It became imperative that we provide a forum for people to voice their fears about what would happen if others—particularly those unfamiliar with how the roles were historically done–began to assume leadership roles. This helped us to get to the root of the dominant group's fear of losing power. Fears were expressed that those in the marginalized group wouldn't let them participate, or that they would do the jobs better than had been done in the past. They also feared that the work of the past would not be appreciated by those doing it in the present. We continually assured the dominant group that they were valued just as much as ever. In fact, they were doing a great thing: They were willing to take a leap of faith, share their power, and pray for those who had the opportunity to try new roles and tasks. Furthermore, the dominant group would also be doing something new: They would be trying roles and tasks that they had not engaged in before. By affirming previous contributions and assuring them that they were needed in the present, we set the foundation for their assistance to move forward in the future.

There also seems to be something inside of us that wants to believe that if we don't do it, then no one else will, or that no one else will be able to do it as well as we can, or even that the church will fall apart if we don't do it. These grandiose tendencies contribute to the dominant group's justification for why they hoard power. At an annual meeting, one member of the dominant group announced that, as he saw it, our church was declining in membership and losing money; furthermore, he predicted we would have to close our doors and merge with another church. The reality is that if any of us are with Jesus tomorrow, the church will continue to function. After all, isn't that the point? The heart of the Christian faith claims that we do what we can for the mission of Christ, and then we let go of this life in order to be with Jesus through eternal life.

We decided that everyone was going to try to do something new in the life of the church. If they were teachers in the public school system and had been teaching Sunday school, then they were invited to handle the financial matters of the church. Those who had been deacons and were concerned about the church's spiritual life could join the building crew for a Habitat for Humanity house. If they had done it all, then we encouraged them to come up with something new and innovative to do for the church. Essentially, everyone took a step to the left and did something they had never before tried. We also instituted a rule between a person who had fulfilled a role in the past and the one currently trying it for the first time: The person new to the position could ask for help from the person who had done the task before, but that person could not offer help. This assured that someone who was willing to try something different had the freedom to do so.

With time, the dominant group became excited about trying new things. They discovered untapped gifts and talents. Because people were now engaged in unfamiliar projects, they spent coffee hour talking to others whom they had not spoken to before. The new tasks led to new relationships, as people had to mobilize others to complete their projects. If one person did a task differently than it had been done in the past, he was not wrong but celebrated for his originality. Instead of a committee model of tasking, we moved to asking people to be on short-term and agenda-specific task forces. When the task was completed, the group disbanded, and the power was returned to the whole.

The director of Christian Education discovered that she had a gift to be the junior high choir director. She asked a parent to help her organize rehearsals, and she continued to have a warm relationship with the children of the church. The junior high choir numerically grew because she had spent so much time nurturing relationships. Eventually she expressed relief that she did not have to continue being an administrator—a job she did not enjoy, but one she feared would not be done by anyone else were she to step down. I was quite pleased to hear that she recently told the new director of Christian Education what a good job she is doing and how she hears such positive feedback from the parents. When the dominant group is able to affirm the participation of the marginalized group, then we know we are witnessing the work of the holy spirit.

Criteria for Power Distribution

In a multicultural church, there are three criteria for distributing power among members in the congregation. One, power is assigned based on role and/or function. Role is defined as a position of "being," and function is a position of "doing." One might serve as the moderator but assign the tasks traditionally associated with such to another group of people. One cannot make a decision that is to be made by the person in that role. For instance, if the Christian Education Committee is discussing which curriculum to implement and disagreement among members arises, a member of the Board of Deacons cannot offer input. In segregated churches, this way of distributing power happens frequently. Those who want to voice their opinion about any matter concerning the life of the church do so, especially during the annual meeting. They assume that they are in a position to give their opinion even though they were not privy to the dialogue about how the decision was reached.

At the same time, members of a committee or task force represent the congregation and should not only have the entire congregation's best interests at heart but, in certain circumstances, should solicit input from the congregation. If it is a major decision, congregational polity warrants that we hold a meeting and allow each person to have a voice. The problem is that not everyone feels as if he or she has an equal voice. Some decisions merely require the approval and prayer of the congregation rather than opinions about whether or not a group of people made the best decision. Some will speak to remind everyone of their power. Others will not say anything because they are shy or reserved, or because they support the decision being made. In some ethnic groupings, silence is a sign not of support, but of dissent.

Like the commandments for the multicultural church, we also found that we need to implement several other rules for group functioning. When someone in a committee or group says, "Well, I think . . . ," they are voicing their own opinion. Some may share that same opinion; others may think differently. The distinction needs to be made when someone on a committee is voicing someone else's opinion. There may be certain instances where is it appropriate to survey the congregation and report the findings back to the committee. Too often, however, the dialogue goes like this: "I heard from fifteen people that they are unhappy with the change." A power struggle commences between committee members until someone inevitably makes the claim, "Well, I heard from twenty people, and they love it!" Another rule is that people are not allowed to voice someone's opinion unless that person has given the committee member permission to use his or her name. Furthermore, leaders need to assess whether or not opinions from those outside the group reflect others' attempts to assume power.

Two, power is assigned to the person performing the task or function only to the extent necessary to complete that specific task.

If I am asked to design a brochure for the outreach program to deliver to the community, I can choose the color, design the layout, and select which photographs depict the exciting things happening in our church. I can write the text, and I might ask other people if I can read it to them for feedback. (Thus I am asking for help.) I can decide whether a picture of the church should go on the front of the brochure and if we should list the church's e-mail address. But I cannot voice my opinion of what the outreach committee should do with the brochure—whether they will hand it out door-to-door, in front of the grocery store, or to visitors on Sunday morning. Unless they ask for my additional help, I cannot offer it. Once the brochure is completed, my power to influence the project has come to an end.

In segregated churches, those who at one time had designed a brochure perceive that they not only have a right to voice their opinion about what I am doing but also to lend their influence and offer help due to their expertise. When I explain that I was thinking about doing something a little different than has been done in the past, I have to worry that they may feel offended. They think they have the right to influence the production of the brochure because, at one time in the distant past, they had the power to complete this same task.

Three, power is sustained based on competency. If a parishioner is struggling to fulfill a task effectively, the church should let the person off the hook. Too often what happens is that the same person is assigned the same function, and year after year it is not done very well, but no one else seems to want the job. If everyone is well aware that the task is not being done well, then no one wants to be in the position of having everyone else judge him or her next. During the time of transition, when centralized power shifts from being hoarded by fifteen people to one person based on the performance of a task, we noted that several of the committees and task forces had vacancies. This reinforces the myth of the dominant group that if they don't do the job, no one else will do it. But with patience and endurance, we found that there was someone waiting to volunteer. If not, maybe the task was no longer needed.

The Pastor's Power

When I call the children forward for a story during worship, the children rush past the adults in the pews, run down the aisle as fast as they can, and vie for position next to the pastor sitting on the chancel. Those who run a little slower or who had to maneuver past a number of adults look quite frustrated and disappointed when they reach the chancel because they have to sit farther away than they hoped. On occasion I have seen one child physically push another child out of the way to secure that favored position. Just like the mother of the sons of Zebedee who wanted her children to be able to sit next to Jesus in the coming kingdom (Matt. 20:20–23), so do the children of the church want to sit next to the pastor. This is because the pastor radiates power.

Adults also have this need, but they (hopefully) contain such desires and seek closeness to the pastor and his or her power in other ways. They may seek out the pastor during coffee hour for conversation or be willing to serve on a task force that the pastor is involved with in order to build a relationship. This need for closeness makes some people vulnerable to being victimized by sexually acting-out clergy. It is the responsibility of the pastor to set the boundaries between themselves and the parishioners. These boundaries are currently being discussed in many clergy circles as a matter of ethics. In most professional relationships, what is known as "dual relationships," that is, friendships, breach the code of ethics.

Some parishioners will attempt to develop a friendship with the pastor. They invite him or her to a social event in their homes. In small-and medium-sized churches, there is often an expectation that the pastor will attend birthday parties, graduations, anniversary celebrations, etc., as well as be present for every fellowship event in the life of the church. The current debate is this: "Can pastors be friends with parishioners?" I will argue that pastors cannot be friends with parishioners in a multicultural church. The reason for this is because pastors have power, and should have power, but they must use that power so that every parishioner feels the same level of closeness.

Pastors represent God. It is not the pastor that people want to feel close to, but God. Because we cannot see God, we build a relationship with a representative of God. Pastors have the power to invoke the presence of God. But a pastor is not God. We are professionals who need to be aware of boundaries between our professional selves and those to whom we minister and develop professional relationships through which parishioners can experience the love of a caring God. Parishioners are not able to project their need for a representative of God onto the pastor when he or she is also a friend. I often say, "I get paid to allow people to project onto me."

Because pastors represent God, they radiate power because God is projected with power. I call this the halo effect. It is an imaginary (that is, it stems from the process of projecting that which originates in one's mind and is transferred onto another person) circle of power that surrounds the pastor's presence. The halo radiates in a physical space around him or her. I explored how this works in chapter three.

When a pastor forms an inner-circle of friends, those friends share in the pastor's power. Because this circle is not open to everyone in the church, parishioners are faced with applying for the position. Like the children trying to sit close to the pastor, adults may subconsciously vie to secure one of these positions in the inner circle, especially those adults who feel powerless in other social settings. This encourages competition among parishioners at the expense of working toward a spirit of cooperation, which is a characteristic of the multicultural church.

Once in the circle, there is an unspoken covenant between pastor and parishioner. The parishioner must be willing to defend the pastor's power. The purpose of the inner circle is to guard the pastor in case of attack. The pastor may intentionally select his or her inner circle because he or she evaluates a potential friend as one who would stand up at a committee meeting and support the pastor's agenda. There is an expectation that the inner circle can be depended upon for this support. The pastor thus invests energy in building a relationship with a parishioner with the hope that this person will protect the pastor from others in the congregation who may challenge his or her power. This is one of the most common ways that a group of parishioners become the dominant group.

However, what often happens is that another group emerges to challenge the power of the past, and that challenge may manifest itself from a criticism to a call for a vote of confidence. If this second group of parishioners gains power and support from others to voice this complaint against the pastor in a form of a letter to sign, then the pastor expects that those in the inner circle should defend him or her. But if those in the inner circle who were initially drawn to the pastor's power perceive that that power is dwindling, they may re-evaluate whether or not they want to be in the inner circle. If the power of the opposing group seems to strengthen and they now appear to have the upper hand, so to speak, those in the inner circle will be attracted to the power of the opposing group. When (not if) that happens, the inner circle will shift its allegiance to the opposing group. As chaff blows in the wind, the inner circle will resign from its position and begin aligning itself with the group that the congregation seems to be investing with power. Meanwhile, the pastor feels hurt and betrayed that his or her so-called friends didn't offer defense when needed the most.

When pastors develop friendships with parishioners, they are enabling and sustaining a dominant group. Most pastor-parish conflict arises because one person instigates others who feel as powerless as he or she does, and together they accumulate some power. One of the most effective ways of getting power in the church is to launch a campaign against the pastor. This often results in a process known as "splitting." Individual parishioners are summoned to choose sides. Tension increases not only in worship but in fellowship events. Some people don't want to get involved, so they simply stop attending church. Once this dysfunction unfolds, it is extremely difficult to alleviate. While some pastors may be called to accountability for actions that are viewed as ineffective or unethical, much conflict could be prevented when pastors draw appropriate boundaries between themselves and parishioners. This holds true among the ethnic groupings.

Pastors of the multicultural movement need to be aware of these boundary issues in order to protect themselves. Many people, especially across ethnic groupings, need to perceive that the pastor is strong and able to defend him or herself. When pastors form friendships for the purpose of protection, some ethnic groupings will perceive this as a sign of weakness. The pastor who communicates a "I can take care of myself" attitude will be in a better position to be perceived as one who can also protect his or her congregation from conflict.

Culturally Diverse Groups Relate Differently to the Pastor's Power

In order to understand how to redistribute power in the multicultural church, Eric Law applies the work of Geert Hofstede, who identifies the perception of power as one of the major differences between ethnic groupings.[3] In some countries, there is a three-tier system of power. At the top of the pyramid are the upper class, who have money, prestige, and privilege. In the middle level is the middle class, who perceive they can access power under certain circumstances. At the bottom level is the lower economic class, who have difficulty accessing power in many social situations. America is an example of this three-tier system. Hofstede refers to this as "the low power distance model" because there is economic mobility between the tiers (e.g., anyone can run for president or lose his or her job and be in poverty tomorrow), and there is not as much difference in the amount of power from one level to the next in the two-tier system.

Other countries adhere to a two-tier system, which Hofstede refers to as "a high power distance model." There are the powerful elite, although few in number, and then there is everyone else. The few elite have tremendous power, but it is assumed that they make decisions with everyone's best interests at heart. For instance, in the ancient world, kings were responsible for the widows and orphans. Several countries in Asia practice this model. Because almost everyone has access to some power, they support the system by respecting and preserving the power of the elite. Essentially, then, almost everyone has the same amount of power.

I find this model helpful to understand how diverse ethnic groups relate differently to the pastor and his or her power. European

Americans tend to perceive that they have the right to voice their opinion in an annual meeting, even if it is a complaint directed to the pastor or a person in power. They might write a letter to the pastor detailing these complaints. In my pastorate, I decided a long time ago not to read letters. I work passionately to develop relationships with parishioners, and therefore do not encourage people to write letters of complaint to people with whom they are in relationship. We can write letters of complaint to our politicians with whom we might have no other way of expressing dissatisfaction. I do allow parishioners to come into my office and read the letter to me, but they cannot put it in the mail, in which case I would have to read it without the opportunity to immediately respond to their concerns. From a pastoral standpoint, I have found that those who are willing to talk about feeling angry are angry at something beyond their initial complaint against the pastor. Had I let them send the letter, this would have been a missed opportunity for me to strengthen our relationship.

Other ethnic groupings perceive complaints about the pastor's performance to be not only disrespectful to the pastor but to the congregation that supports him or her. In high-power distant cultures, such as the Philippines, no one would dare take on the powerful elite. Because in the Asian American community the pastor represents God and radiates God's power, the pastor is viewed as in the upper tier, the elite. They might ask themselves, if the pastor thinks it should be done this way, who am I to question his or her authority? Those who do question or challenge that authority are not only attacking the pastor but also the community. European Americans emphasize the individual, whereas other ethnic groupings focus on the collective. If one challenges the power of an individual who represents the collective, then it is the collective who are under attack. In the Asian American community, then, defending the honor of the pastor is equated with defending the honor of the church.

Summary

The focus of this chapter was deconstructing the centralized power model that is characteristic of the segregated church. Fifteen people draw a boundary around themselves and form a dominant group that hoards power. Those who become overly involved in the church and/or claim a long history of membership are candidates to become friends with the pastor. When the pastor allows for an inner circle to develop with the hope that this group will defend him or her in case of attack, he or she is enabling the unequal distribution of power in the congregation.

I offer a new model that decentralizes power and shares it based on role. Power is correlated with performance. In other words, you have to do a task effectively (and this is a subjective measurement) in order to continue in that role. But you cannot have that role very long because there are other people in the church who want to assuage it. In this model, I suggest that the dominant group take a leap of faith and try new roles and tasks in the life of the congregation, allowing for those in the marginalized group to take on new tasks as well. I propose that the two-tier model of "high distance" between pastor and parishioners may serve the multicultural church more effectively than a middle tier, where some people can access power, and a lower tier, where others cannot. Pastors need to be aware of the process whereby parishioners project power onto them in order to be able to use it to everybody's advantage. By redistributing power throughout the congregation, the idolatry that some people are more important to the life of the congregation than others is melted away.

CHAPTER SEVEN

View of the Promised Land

Envisioning the Multicultural Church

TWENTY YEARS AGO, I led a work camp for Habitat for Humanity in Haiti. One day when I was sitting in a restaurant eating a chicken sandwich, a young man came in, walked up to the counter, and ordered a chicken sandwich. I had never seen him before, but he immediately caught my attention because he was white. "What group are you with?" I yelled over to him. He answered, "Water for Life. And you?" I responded, "Habitat for Humanity." Back then, the only white people walking around Haiti were affiliated with missionary organizations. He got his chicken sandwich and sat down at the table while I finished mine. It was so good to have someone to talk with in English, as I had grown tired of struggling to speak Creole. I missed seeing other Americans, and this was an opportunity to catch up on what was happening in the United States. In this land, where everyone seemed to do things differently, it was a welcome relief to find someone like me. The experience gave me some insight into what it must be like to dwell in a land with different cultural norms from one's land of origin. I also now understand why immigrants feel a need to worship together and to preserve, and pass on to their children, the cultural traditions of their homeland.

As the shift began to occur from being a segregated church to becoming a multicultural one, several of us noticed that, while we all worshiped together in one sanctuary, there was a tendency for ethnic groupings to sit near each other. We also noted that persons from the same ethnic grouping tended to sit at the same table during church suppers. Initially, multicultural leaders were concerned that we were not integrating to become multicultural. One expectation was that persons from diverse ethnic groups should be integrated into every aspect of church life. But we came to appreciate we are created with a natural tendency to flock to people like ourselves. Instead of trying to suppress this part of our created being, we soon realized that we had to find ways to honor it.

Within the body of Christ, groups develop naturally—what we call "cell groups." A multicultural church not only fosters opportunities for these groups to form but provides structure for some of them, e.g., Bible study for the gay and lesbian community. A multicultural church does everything it can to encourage the preservation of cultural traditions and to build solidarity within specific cultural groupings. But at the same time, a multicultural church works to facilitate the building of relationships with persons from other cultural groupings. Honoring and respecting our diversity is key. And yet, coming together as one body to worship God and finding common ground is just as important to us. We balance our need to be in relationship with people who share our cultural grouping with our need to be in relationship with brothers and sisters in Christ.

Because multiculturalism is a relatively new subject to study in relation to the Christian church, the present task before us is to construct a model for others to follow. For a model to be effective, it has to have three criteria: One, it has to fit with our understanding of cultural distribution; that is, the power has to be decentralized and distributed between cultural groupings. Two, it has to encourage relationship building between cultural groupings and individuals. Three, it has to move us further in the journey to become a multicultural church and not simply get us stuck in any one place along the way.

The Renting Model

Several churches are renting their sanctuary or fellowship hall for worship to another church. On the surface, this seems to benefit both churches because the host church makes a little extra money and the guest church finds a place to worship. The host church might even be willing to allow the guest church to announce their presence to the neighborhood with a secondary sign out front. They exist as independent churches in one building and do not share in worship, often for the reason that the guest church is affiliated with a different denomination from the host church or conducts their worship service in a different language.

The first problem I see with this model is that the host church is the dominant group simply because they own the church. The guest church has to accommodate the needs of the host church, such as worship time, or when, in the words of the host church, "our sanctuary is not being used." The guest church is welcome to use the worship space for as long as the host church perceives that they (the host church) are benefiting from this economic arrangement. If the guest church finds themselves unable to pay their rent one month, they might need to ask the host church for an extension. Whether or not this extension is granted is the privilege of the host church.

I know of one situation where the guest church is growing numerically, attracting new people and families with children. The music is inspirational and lively and appeals to the young generation. The host church has an average attendance of fifteen people and rents its sanctuary because membership and finances have been declining. They see all the cars in the parking lot and have become resentful toward the guest church. The host church resents that the community is responding to the guest church and cannot understand why they do not come to its worship service. The pastor of the guest church shared with me that the sexton often does his vacuuming during their worship service. Recently, the host church announced that the rent was going to double. Their rationale: If the guest church is growing, then they should have more money to pay more rent and help support the increased use of the church building.

The renting model also often presupposes that the host church is of one ethnic grouping and the guest church is of another. The host church tends to be European Americans and guest churches today tend to be Hispanic American, Haitian American and Asian American. The host church, as representative of the dominant group, then hoards power from the guest church, who may feel helpless to complain against these problems, as they are dependent upon the host church for worship space. The guest church feels at the mercy of the host church for fear of displacement and having to find another worship space. This model represents an unequal distribution of power between the two groups and therefore reflects some of the same social problems currently plaguing the segregated European American church.

I will argue against the renting model. The unequal distribution of power is but one problem among many. Several years ago, when I was approached by a Haitian American pastor to rent worship space, I told him that we do not own the church. This church belongs to Jesus. We are merely stewards of the church building. Therefore, it is not ours to rent. Secondly, the argument often used in favor of the renting model is language. For those who do not speak English, they need a pastor who speaks the language of their land of origin. While I am sensitive to this issue, I do not see it as a long-term one. The children of immigrants will be more likely to learn English, especially those growing up in our educational system. To base church starts, then, on the cultural preservation of language, may meet the needs of the present generation, but perhaps be less important to the next. I respect that it is important to some parents to teach their children the language of their homeland, but this might not be the basis for a separate, segregated church when they reach adulthood. These children might be more interested in worshiping with their friends from other ethnic groupings. Thus, the renting model is not a long-term strategy toward becoming a multicultural church. In some instances, it might serve as a transition.

The Sister Church Model

Another model is the sister church model. A church that is located in the suburbs and comprised primarily of European Americans links itself with a sister church located in the inner city whose membership is a different ethnic background. While both churches are segregated, they share community meals and fellowship events that allow for relationship building. I am in favor of this model if it is viewed as an objective leading to becoming a multicultural, multiracial church located somewhere in between. My concern is that this will allow each church to continue to function as a segregated church and not pursue the next step. I am also concerned that the congregation who initiates the interaction is also most often the church comprised of European Americans. Because they represent the dominant group, they may cause their sister church to feel uneasy about voicing any opposition to their efforts.

The Integration Model

Another Haitian American pastor and a few members of his church approached me recently because they had heard that our church is in the process of becoming multicultural. The discussion focused on integrating the two churches. We decided that we would offer two worship services: I would preach in the nine o'clock service. As we have several other pastors who also lead worship, the Haitian American pastor would join our worship team. At the eleven o'clock service (not called first or second service as if there is a hierarchy of preference), the Haitian American pastor will preach the sermon in Creole with a translator. Because the children in the Haitian American church speak English, their parents wanted them to attend Sunday school in a multicultural church. It is promoted that all persons affiliated with the church are welcome to attend either worship service. Maintaining only one Sunday school would allow us to accomplish this integration. In a recent survey, most people selected a service based on "convenience of time" rather than because they preferred to hear one pastor preach.

This model is still in the planning stages. The risk in this endeavor is that the Haitian Americans will only attend the service when the Haitian American pastor preaches. But I am not too concerned about this, as people with children who speak English will attend the nine o'clock service when Sunday school is taught. Because that service is multiracial and there are already Haitian Americans in attendance, some will feel comfortable attending this service from the start. Two reasons we need two services:

One, the nine o'clock service is already full, and two, we need a service when the sermon is preached in Creole. This will meet the needs of what the pastor refers to as "the little old ladies" who insist that the sermon be delivered in Creole, but who speak enough English to listen to the pastors of the multicultural church speak in English during other parts of the service.

To bring the reader up to date, this marks where we are in the process of becoming a multicultural church. We have not yet implemented the plan of integration, which is set for Lent of 2006. There has been much dialogue and excitement about the upcoming merger. We have tried to anticipate potential problems and formed a committee of representatives from each of the committees in the church in order to try to put some structure on how this will work. We did not want to just say, "Come and be part of us" without putting in place an intentional process so as to reduce the potential for problems. Both pastors are well aware that problems will emerge, so we are trying to anticipate them and agree upon how to resolve them.

Characteristics of the Multicultural Church

First Congregational Church of Randolph is still roaming in the wilderness. While we have achieved a multiethnic membership, we are well aware that most churches continue to practice segregation. Recently, a group of people in the church approached me about rewriting our mission statement. Because we know that God will not let us onto the promised land until all churches become multicultural, this group was concerned that perhaps our work now is to trying to convince others churches that they need to engage in this process.

As Christians, we want other churches to experience what we have experienced and what we know to be God's plan for the future of the body of Christ. There is a great responsibility that comes with being a model church. Many of our members drive quite a distance (some from another state) in order to participate in what they feel is an exciting, faithful, and spiritually uplifting experience. They are out witnessing to this experience and encouraging friends and neighbors to drive from their neighborhoods, out of their comfort zone, to take a leap of faith and experience the joy that comes from worshiping in a culturally diverse community. Those who have this experience find they do not want to return to a segregated faith community because they know they are participating in building God's kingdom here on earth.

In a multicultural church, people are not inner-focused on meeting their own spiritual needs 100 percent of the time. With an open mind and heart, I might find that a cultural tradition from the Korean American church speaks to my spirituality in a way that I might not have anticipated. I would not have had this moment of self-discovery had I been in a segregated church that narrowly sought to meet the spiritual needs of the ethnic grouping present in worship. Myself, I cannot stand some of the contemporary Christian punk music, but I tap my foot and try to get into the beat and let the holy spirit dance within me. I also cannot stand singing the traditional hymn, "Rock of Ages," but when we sing it, I try to put these feelings aside. When the praise band sings, "Jesus is Just Alright With Me" by the Doobie Brothers, I am in my spiritual glory. But I am also aware that there are others who are tapping their feet. What is important to those who worship in a multicultural church is that the diversity of worshipers transforms the worship, often in unexpected ways, and that wonder and mystery take priority over likes and dislikes with respect to worship styles and musical preferences.

Another characteristic of the multicultural congregation is that we draw a boundary around ourselves as Christians. Multiculturalism, as a subject for study in relation to the church, does not seek to evangelize persons from other faiths. Initially, some worried that if we became a multicultural church, we would no longer be a church that identified itself as a United (and Uniting) Church of Christ. Whereas membership honors those with respect to ethnicity and race, gender, age, class, ability, and sexual preference, we intentionally did not add "religious affiliation." What defines us as "us" is that we are sisters and brothers in Christ. The "other" is categorized as those from other religious faith communities.

A third characteristic of the multicultural church is its spirit of cooperation rather than competition. As numbers dwindle, churches are forced to compete to attract new parishioners. It is also considered acceptable to "steal" a parishioner from one's sister church. Instead of returning a lost sheep to its flock, a church that is experiencing low morale and financial woes might be tempted to warmly welcome the lost sheep into its fold. This, however, is a more complicated problem. People who tend to leave one church for another often have a pattern of conflict that gets replayed in each church setting. They may come complaining about the pastor down the street, but with time, will find themselves voicing those same complaints about the pastor in the church they currently attend.

It has also been my experience that male pastors tend to enable parishioners who are unwilling to try to accept a female pastor. When I arrived at each of the four churches that I have served, there were some people who voiced their opinion that they did not think women should be ministers. Instead of giving the pastor-parishioner relationship a chance, they went screaming to a neighboring church where the male pastor welcomed and comforted them and provided a refuge so that they could stay there until she's gone. These pastors do not realize that they are enabling prejudice against women and sabotaging efforts to become a multicultural church.

There is also evidence of competition among pastors themselves. Whenever I am with colleagues I don't know very well, someone inevitably asks me, "So how big is your church?" I'm not sure what it is we are actually comparing. There is an underlying assumption that the numerically larger a church one serves, the better the pastor is who serves it. We have to wonder whether or not the conferences set up this situation as area ministers tend to pay more attention to pastors who serve numerically large churches. Further, those who have historically worked for the conferences in positions of power have been European American men. Hopefully, things will begin to change so that the United Church of Christ will continue to attract persons from other cultural groupings. As the pastoral leadership in our churches becomes more culturally diverse, so will our membership.

The Goals of the Multicultural Church

When the church shifts its way of distributing power, it models for the community a different way of doing things. For instance, I have been the first female pastor in all four churches I have served. After I was called to one of these churches, a parishioner from another church in town commented to me, "We're thinking about calling a woman pastor, too, because we realize that after your church called you, it didn't fall apart." She expresses the fear of many that redistributing power to those who have not historically been allowed access to it may result in their abusing it. I often feel that women pastors have to be twice as effective as male pastors because we have something to prove; that is, that we are capable of leading a congregation.

There are three goals of the multicultural church:

1. to model for the community a social system that equally distributes power among its members and still functions well;

2. to convince other institutions, including other churches, to become multicultural by example; and

3. to transfer new patterns of relating to persons of various ethnic backgrounds to these other institutions.

The objective for the multicultural church is to teach parishioners and the church as a system new patterns of relating to persons of other cultural groupings. Within the church setting, during worship, fellowship, and mission projects, individuals develop relationships and challenge and change their perception of themselves and others. They confront their fears concerning their interactions with people who are different from themselves; by reality-testing these fears and discovering that they have no basis in reality, they let go of them. The opposite of love in not hate or indifference, but fear of the Other. As persons from diverse cultural groupings have an opportunity to interact and build relationships, to love and to laugh, they experience the benefits of being in a multicultural environment. Often, those who were resistant find themselves repenting their fears and so function as witnesses for others who may continue to harbor fear and doubt.

The goal for the multicultural church is to apply these new insights to their interactions with friends, neighbors, and strangers on the street. In essence, parishioners practice these new patterns of interaction in a controlled environment where multicultural leaders model appropriate patterns and confront those that promote or sustain prejudice. The strategy is to transfer what they learn in the church to the way that they treat other people in the community. Because our attitude about people's cultural grouping determines our behavior, or how we relate to them, the objective is to change people's attitudes with the hope and prayer that their behavior will change as well.

"The end or the goal of multiculturalism should not be increased sensitivity or inclusivism so that no one is locked outside the gate.... Rather, it should be to see the church, by the way of multiethnicity, inclusivism and cultural sensitivity, bring about biblical reconciliation, justice and righteousness in the church *and in society*.[11] (Emphasis added.) The purpose of the Christian church is to model for society patterns of relating which fight against prejudice and promote justice. If this transfer of learning in relation to society does not take place, then the journey to become the multicultural church will not bear fruit.

Jesus commissions all Christians to model for society these patterns of relating. "Go therefore and make disciples of all nations, baptizing them in the name of the Father and of the Son and of the Holy Spirit" (Matt. 28:19). The Greek word *ethnos* is translated here as "nations," but it can also be translated as "ethnicities" or "ethnic groupings." Becoming the multicultural and multiethnic church is not an option that some churches will engage in because they are located in multiethnic neighborhoods and others will remain segregated. It is a biblical mandate that we are to go out into the world and evangelize it by intentionally working toward bringing a diversity of ethnic groupings into the body of Christ. My hope and prayer is that all who hear these words will go out into the world and do likewise.

Notes

Introduction

1. This information is according to the 2005 Massachusetts census.

2. Because intermarriage between persons of different races has become more socially acceptable, many children are biracial and even multiracial.

3. E. D. Hirsch, Jr., Joseph F. Kett, and James Trefil, *Dictionary of Cultural Literacy*, 2d ed. (Boston: Houghton Mifflin, 1993), 415.

4. Michael V. Angrosino, *Talking About Cultural Diversity in your Church: Gifts and Challenges* (Walnut Creek, Georgia: AltaMira Press, 2001), 9.

5. Arne Fritson and Samuel Kabue, *Interpreting Disability: A Church of All for All* (Geneva, Switzerland: World Council of Churches Publication, 2004), x.

Chapter 1: And the Lord Sent Plagues: *Problems Afflicting the Segregated European American Community*

1. All quotations are from the *New Revised Standard Version*, unless my own translation.

2. Eric H. F. Law, writes, "Over the years, I have learned that by focusing on the powerful few, I was actually reaffirming their power and influence and that my engagement with the powerful with my power would only serve to disempower the rest of the community members, who would then become powerless observers." *The Word at the Crossing: Living the Good News in a Multicultural Community* (St. Louis, Mo.: Chalice Press, 2004), 60.

3. Liston Pope, *The Kingdom Beyond Caste* (New York: Friendship Press, 1957), 105.

4. Stephen Rhodes, *Where Nations Meet: The Church in a Multicultural World* (Downers Grove: InterVarsity Press, 1998), 17.

5. Unfortunately, when the denomination that owned the church got wind of what we were doing, they were afraid that the new members might be more loyal to the United Church of Christ and vote to leave the denomination. So they provided pastoral leadership for the church.

6. Rick Rusaw and Eric Swanson, *The Externally Focused Church* (Loveland, Colo.: Group, 2004).

Chapter 3: The Burning Bush: Multicultural Images of God

1. Sigmund Freud, *Moses and Monotheism* (New York: Vintage Books, 1939).
2. Phyllis Trible, *God and the Rhetoric of Sexuality* (Philadelphia: Fortress Press, 1978).
3. The technical term for this literary device is *merismus*.
4. For instance, Exodus 14:19, "The angel of God who was going before the Israelite army moved and went behind them; and the pillar of cloud moved from in front of them and took its place behind them."
5. David Anderson, *Multicultural Ministry: Finding Your Church's Unique Rhythm* (Grand Rapids, Mich.: Zondervan, 2004).
6. Ana Maria Rizzuto, *The Birth of the Living God: A Psychoanalytic Study* (Chicago: University of Chicago Press, 1979).

Chapter 5: Revelation at Mt. Sinai: Ten Commandments for the Multicultural Church

1. Eric H. F. Law, *The Wolf Shall Dwell with the Lamb: A Spirituality for Leadership in a Multicultural Community* (St. Louis: Chalice Press, 1993), 2–3.
2. James Cone, *God of the Oppressed* (New York: Seabury Press, 1975), 226.
3. In the literature, this is known as "colorblindness," but with respect for those who cannot physically see color, I will use "denial of difference" to describe the same phenomenon.
4. Peter Wagner, *Our Kind of People: The Ethical Dimensions of Church Growth in America* (Atlanta: John Knox Press, 1979), 60.
5. Tony Matthews, *There's More Than One Color in the Pew: A Handbook for Multicultural, Multiracial Churches* (Macon: Smyth & Helwys, 2003), 76ff.
6. Duane Elmer, *Cross-Cultural Conflict: Building Relationships for Effective Ministry* (Downers Grove: InterVarsity Press, 1993), p. 30
7. Anderson, *Multicultural Ministry*.

Chapter 6: Melting the Golden Calf: *The Redistribution of Power*

1. Jung Young Lee, *Marginality: The Key to Multicultural Theology* (Minneapolis: Fortress, Press, 1995), 45.
2. Eric H. F. Law, *The Word at the Crossings: Living the Good News in a Multicultural Community* (St. Louis, Chalice Press, 2004), 62.
3. Geert Hofstede, *Culture's Consequences: International Differences in Work-Related Values* (Beverly Hills: Sage Publications, 1987).

Chapter 7: A View of the Promised Land: *Envisioning the Multicultural Church*

1. Manuel Ortiz, *One New People: Models for Developing a Multiethnic Church* (Downers Grove: InterVarsity Press, 1996), p. 60.

Appendix A

Seasons of the Church Year

CHRISTIANS FIRST CELEBRATED the birth of Jesus on January 6 and called it "Epiphany" because God was revealing something new. Not until 325 CE, in another part of the world, did December 25 become the date for celebrating Jesus' birth. The winter solstice festival was traditionally held on that day, and church officials wanted to replace it with a Christian celebration. The twelve days of Christmas, also known as "Christmastide," is the period from the new feast day (December 25) to the old feast day (January 6). In many Latin American countries, January 6 is the day for giving presents.

Advent is the period leading up to Christmas and marks the start of the church year. It began in France as a six-week season of preparation for baptism. In the sixth century, this was shortened to the four Sundays before Christmas, beginning on the Sunday nearest Saint Andrew's Day, November 30. The focus switched to being a preparation for the birth of Jesus. Advent today is a period of quiet waiting, anticipation, and sometimes fasting before the celebration begins on the evening of December 24. Advent traditions vary from place to place, depending upon the culture.

The colors of the season are violet, purple, and blue. Some churches use rose as the color on the third Sunday because of the lighter tone to the traditional reading on that day (Phil. 4:4: "Rejoice in God"). Some of the more popular traditions include the use of Advent wreaths, logs, calendars, stars, and the placing of lights in windows.

Advent is a season of preparing for the birth of Jesus into the world and for a rebirth in our lives. It is a time of awe and wonder, a time of receiving the good news so deeply into our hearts, minds, and souls that we become more Christlike. It is a time of offering the joy and hope we feel to a world that so desperately needs the investment and involvement of ourselves. Advent also gives us a hint of what is to come in Jesus' life. Some traditions place a heavy emphasis on self-examination and repentance, on preparing for the second coming, when Christ will come in judgment. This adds a somber note to the birthday festivities, and sometimes we simply need to celebrate.

During the Christmas season, the world remembers the incarnation of Christ, God's taking on of human form. The Christmas season includes a number of special days. These honor Saint Stephen, the first Christian martyr; Saint John, the apostle and evangelist; and the holy innocents killed in Bethlehem because of Jesus' birth. The color for the season is white.

Worship services on Christmas Eve and Christmas Day vary. Some churches have a "Lessons and Carols" service early on Christmas Eve, designed for families with young children. Others hold a more liturgical service around midnight. Some meet on Christmas Day for their main Christmas service.

Epiphany was originally an Eastern festival that celebrated both the incarnation and the baptism of Jesus on January 6. In the West, the focus came to be on the arrival of the Magi (the three kings). The baptism of Jesus is then observed on the Sunday following Epiphany.

Many cultures have their own traditional ways of celebrating Advent, Christmas, and Epiphany. In Hispanic traditions, festivities generally begin on December 16 and end on January 6. The nine days preceding Christmas represent the nine months that Mary was pregnant with Jesus. On each of these days, the drama of Las Posadas (the inns) is enacted on the city streets. This daily drama tells the story of Joseph and Mary looking for a place to stay in Bethlehem and being repeatedly turned away.

After the celebrations of Christmas Eve and Christmas Day slow down, the festivities of Los Pastores (the shepherds) are held in early January. This folk drama, which depicts the shepherds' travel to Bethlehem to see the Christ child, actually is a means of teaching Bible stories and lessons of faith. The arrival of the Magi is celebrated on January 6.

In Mexico the first two weekends in December are the time of the Fiesta de las Luminarias, the lighting of the Holy Family's way to Bethlehem, often illustrated by lining walkways with candles inside paper bags filled with sand. December 12 is also celebrated in Mexico as the day the Virgin of Guadalupe appeared.

Many cultures use traditional objects for celebrating Advent, Christmas, and Epiphany. These include:

ADVENT CALENDAR: This is generally a Christmas scene printed on cardboard, with punch-out windows scattered around the picture. One window is opened each day to reveal another picture underneath—something symbolic of Christmas or the Christmas story, like an ornament or presents.

ADVENT CRECHE/PUTT SCENE: This grouping of figurines depicts either the scene in the manger or the entire nativity story, complete with hillsides, sheep, camels, deserts, a moving star, and so on. Some churches read scripture and sing hymns while tiny spotlights follow the course of the narration on the putz. (See the Christmas putz story that appears later in this appendix.)

ADVENT CROSS: The Tau cross, which is in the shape of a T, is said to look like the staff Moses put up for healing. It has come to symbolize the birth of Jesus as the great healer.

ADVENT LOG: Involving the same symbolism as the Advent wreath, the log has a candle for each Sunday of Advent. These candles are lined up in a row instead of in a circle.

ADVENT ROSE: This wild rose blooms in Palestine at the same time each year. It is used to symbolize the faithfulness of God in keeping the promise to send a Savior.

ADVENT STAR: This is a three-dimensional star made out of paper points and illuminated from the inside by an electric bulb. The Moravians began making these in the 1850s, and now they are used by Christians around the world. They generally range in size from one-foot-tall models used in homes to five-foot versions used in church sanctuaries.

ADVENT WREATH: This is a ring of evergreens on which are placed four purple candles (or three purple candles and one rose-colored one); a fifth candle, white, is placed in the center. The circular shape of the wreath stands for the unending love of God. The evergreens (or holly and laurel) represent the immortality and new life found in Christ.

The light of the candles reminds us of Jesus, the Light of the world. Purple has always been considered a royal color and symbolizes the coming sovereignty of Jesus. Purple, or violet, also represents our humility. Sometimes churches assign each candle a specific meaning within a theme. One grouping includes the prophets, shepherds, angels, and Magi. Another grouping includes hope, peace, love, and joy. On Christmas Day, the white Christ candle in the center of the wreath is lit, representing the perfection of Christ.

CHRISTMAS TREE: Although the use of evergreens was used by pre-Christians to stand for everlasting life, it was adopted by Christians to symbolize the life found in Christ.

JESSE TREE: This is a tree hung with emblems representing the genealogy of Jesus. Often the emblems are made out of wood.

POINSETTIA: According to one story, a young Mexican girl wanted to give a present to baby Jesus. An angel told her to pick some green weeds along the road and present them to Jesus in the church. As she did so, the weeds turned into flame-red flowers.

WINDOW LIGHTS: This tradition was adopted by the Moravians, who used beeswax candles. Putting lights in the windows of one's home signaled an openness to the Christ child and to travelers, inviting all to come in for something warm to drink.

Appendix B

Advent Liturgies

Words of Preparation

Join with us, Christ, in this hour of worship. Lift us out of the routine of our daily lives and set us up on your holy mountain. Let our worship come from our hearts; that it may be genuine. Let our praises for you leap from our mouths, that we may be alive with faith and joy. Make us fresh again!

Call to Worship

Walking in the Light

ISAIAH 2:1–5

One:	What do you want from Christmas?
Many:	We want this Christmas to be perfect.
One:	How are you going to make that happen?
Many:	We are going to go up on the mountain of God and learn God's ways. We will put away our drunkenness, quarrels, and addictions. We will beat our swords into plowshares.
One:	It is time to become fully awake.
Many:	It is time to walk in God's light.

Voices of Christmas: Repentance

ISAIAH 11:1–10

One: Where are the voices that lead us to faith in Christ?

Many: In the wilderness where people like John the Baptist are calling out "Repent!"

One: Where are the voices that call us to justice and hope?

Many: In our streets, where people like Martin Luther King Jr. and Dorothy Day call into question the comfort of our lives.

One: The voices of repentance, the voices of justice. You hear the voices. What are you going to do?

Many: We are going to turn our lives around and live for Christ.

Healing and Forgiveness

ISAIAH 35:1–10

One: Prepare the dry land of your hearts for the coming of Jesus!

Many: We hear the cry of the oppressed and the suffering.

One: Prepare the wilderness of your lives for deliverance!

Many: We feel the brokenness that is inside us.

One: Prepare for your dreams to be fulfilled!

Many: God will come down and live among people, and we will sing songs of freedom. We will bind up our aching knees, go to the people of all nations, and work for their liberation.

Fulfillment and Joy

Psalm 24

One:	Do we feel like people who are full of joy and excitement?
Many:	Do you mean like "Christmas people"?
One:	Do we feel closer to God because of the Christmas celebrations this year?
Many:	Are we supposed to?
One:	Who will be with Christ?
Many:	Those who have clean hands and pure hearts.
One:	What does that mean?
Many:	That those who want to be near God will be.
One:	Do you want this?
Many:	We do.
One:	Then let us worship and celebrate the pregnancy of a young woman and the coming fulfillment of all our dreams.

Watching

Psalm 130:6

One:	God calls us to watch, to stand on the city walls and see what is coming, as sentinels watch for the dawn. But what are we to watch for?
Many:	We're watching for the bus at Fourteenth and Broadway. We're watching for our children to come home. We're watching for the coming of Christ's power into the world and our lives, and opportunities for us to share this energy with others.

One:	Anything else?
Many:	We're watching for the signs of peace and justice in a world of much hardness and injustice. And we're watching our rulers to see if they see the signs of change.
One:	Is that all you watch?
Many:	We also watch television and see the struggles going on around the world. It leaves us feeling powerless, guilty, and sad to think that people can treat the rest of God's children with such hatred and violence.
One:	But watching for God is not the same as watching television.
Many:	So how do we watch with despair staring us in the face and not be overcome? How do we watch with feelings of powerlessness and still keep our hope?
One:	We do so by going out into the world and watching Christ move through our words and actions into the lives of others.

Waiting

2 PETER 3:8–15A

One:	In anticipation we gather.
Many:	With expectations we wait.
One:	We gather to watch for the coming of the good news into our world and into our lives.
Many:	We wait to see the fullness of God's vision.
One:	O God, open the doors to our hearts that this year we may have room for the birth of Jesus.

Many:	O God, as we marvel over all that you are doing, overwhelm us with so much wonder that words of praise spring forth from our lips!
One:	In this time of waiting, let true worship begin in our hearts.
Many:	Let our praises rise up to the heavens! Let our celebrations spread new hope over a tired world! Let us gather all our dreams and lives together and worship our God! Amen.

Witness

Psalm 24:3–5; Romans 1:1–7

One:	We are all called to witness to God, yet there are a variety of ways in which we do this.
Many:	We witness by believing that this birth really happened, by believing that what the Scriptures say about Jesus is true.
One:	We witness by living lives that express our beliefs—living with clean hands, pure hearts, and by not committing our souls to what is false and temporary.
Many:	We witness by sharing with others, through what we say and do, just how important Jesus' birth is to us.
One:	As servants of God striving to be saints, we have agreed to live lives of great compassion and mercy, completely dedicated to the work of God.
Many:	We need to take care, however we witness, that we do not let our good intentions get ahead of the Spirit's plans, for it is the Holy Spirit that touches the hearts of others.

Wonder

EXODUS 15:11

One:	Do we feel wonder anymore when we talk about the birth of Jesus? Do we have any sense of awe that God would decide to become human?
Many:	We do find it hard to feel any wonder. Every few years science makes possible what we thought was impossible. But on the spiritual level, nothing seems to change.
One:	So how do we recapture the wonder of this birth?
Many:	By starting with this birth, and seeing where it leads.

Prepare

BARUCH 5:1–9

One:	Prepare the way! Level every mountain! Fill in every valley! Make the road smooth, for royalty is coming.
Many:	What can we do? We don't own any machines big enough to move mountains. We have only shovels.
One:	Then take your shovels to the roads that run through your lives. Smooth out the bumps. Fill in the potholes. Clear the brush that has grown up along the sides.
Many:	We can do that. But what difference will it make?
One:	The changes may seem small to you. But Christ isn't coming in a great presidential motorcade. Christ is coming on a bicycle, stopping here and there among us to chat, to share a meal, to borrow a warm coat for the night.

Many:	We want Christ to dwell among us, so we will change our ways and care for those around us as if they were Christ.
One:	Prepare the way this day for Christ's coming!

Rejoicing

ZEPHANIAH 3; PHILIPPIANS 4

One:	Sing aloud, O daughter of Zion! Shout, O son of Israel! Rejoice and exalt with all your heart!
Many:	God is in our midst! We shall fear disaster no more!
One:	God will heal the infirm and gather the outcast!
Many:	God will change our shame into praise!
One:	You who suffer through no fault of your own; you who have trouble seeing, talking, hearing, and walking; you whose bodies don't fit society's ideals; you who don't feel completely understood or accepted; you whose interests and skills don't bring enough money to make you a "success"; you who respond with your hearts before your heads, and feel ashamed because of this; and all you who hold fast to God when so much of society says religion is irrelevant....
Many:	For all of us who don't feel we measure up because of who we are and what we believe, and who have felt ashamed and suffered because of this....
One:	For your perseverance and faith in matters greater and deeper than what can be seen, God will bring you home with joy, as hostages who return from captivity in a foreign country. Do not grow weary. Do not let your hearts grow weak, for God has come and is in our midst!

Peace

LUKE 1:39–55

Reader 1:	Mary treasured everything the shepherds said about Jesus but pondered how it was going to be possible.
Reader 2:	"This child will establish a world of peace and justice, a world filled with righteousness!"
Many:	This child? The one lying in the feeding bin?
Reader 1:	This child, the one with humble beginnings.
Reader 2:	"A child has been born for us! And the rod of the oppressor will be broken! The yoke of repression will be lifted!"
Many:	It's been two thousand years since this child fulfilled the promises. Does this look like a world of peace?
Reader 1:	At least now such a world of peace is possible.
Reader 2:	"The people who live in a land of deep shadows have seen a great light!" And all who come after this child and believe become the child's hands, feet, and voice in this world.
Many:	You mean us, the ones squirming in the pews?
Reader 1:	If you take the first step, even a baby step, then all miracles become possible!
Many:	Then so be it!
Reader 2:	Amen!

Call to Confession

We cannot come before God unless we are first honest with ourselves about who we are, about the mistakes we make, and how well or how poorly we care for others. In this spirit, let us offer our prayers to God.

Unison Prayers

Holy Spirit, as we prepare ourselves this Advent, be with us and restrain us from trying to do everything. Kindle within us an unquenchable desire to be with you. Do we want to prepare? Do we want to start a serious walk of faith again? O Spirit, take that one thought of renewal within our many doubts and make it grow within us like the first light of dawn. Amen.

Spirit of the desert, the voice of John the Baptist shouting in the wilderness is not the voice we like to hear. After all, we've already repented once. Yet we sense that John knew repentance only goes so far. It's what we do afterward that develops the heart of faith. O God, grant us the courage to truly change and live out our convictions every day. Amen.

We are going to go up on your mountain, dear God. We are going to hear your words and learn your ways. We will take our actions and words that tear people down and turn them into what will tear down the walls that keep us from caring for one another. We will listen and learn. We will study and live your wisdom. Help us hike up your holy mountain! Touchable God, will we feel like Christmas people this year? Will we want to affirm what is good in the world even in the midst of so much that doesn't seem to be going well? Are we ready to be open to people in a way that allows us to help one another get along? Can we let this Christmas be this Christmas, and not some Christmas from the past or one that exists only in our dreams? We're not sure. We feel confused so much of the time. We don't feel ready. What do we want this year? What are our expectations? O God, we have so many questions for you today. Help us settle our minds and listen to our hearts. Help us prepare to receive your joy without reservation.

Potter God, return us as clay to the potter to be re-formed, to have our excesses and accumulations taken off, to be refired in the kiln of your love. God of the rhythm that moves through creation, return us to our homes, to the places of our families' nurturing, that we may reclaim our dreams. Help us travel back to our spiritual homelands, to the tribes of our heritage, that we may bring the rhythms of their songs into our hearts. Amen.

Ubiquitous God, we wait for so many things. We are a needy people. We wait for you to teach us wisdom. We wait for you to show us how to walk humbly upon your way. We wait for you to help us with our personal problems and to administer justice in our often unjust world. Sometimes it seems that all we do is wait for matters to get better, and sometimes we become weary of waiting. Yet we believe, with Isaiah, that our waiting is almost over. The One who will bring light to our shadows, warmth to our cold, and hope to our future is about to be born. As we prepare for the birth this year, may we wait with a patience that is open to new ways. May we wait with a hope that is hard to tear down. May we wait upon the city walls through the solitude of the night and feel our hearts leap when we see the beginnings of dawn on the horizon. Amen.

Mother, we know you have appointed us to bring glad tidings to the afflicted, to proclaim the time of God's favor, to work so hard that we are called oaks of righteousness. Yet can we proclaim and do your word if we are not ourselves set free, or fed, or comforted? Give us the courage to comfort when we are in mourning, for then we will truly understand sadness and loss, and our words will come from the depths of our hearts. When we are hungry, let us feed others first, allowing those around us to see our needs and the opportunity to minister to us in your name. Thus we may know true hunger and true gratitude. Amen.

Eternal One beyond understanding, the deeper we move into your mystery by saying "yes" to your ways, the more we are amazed that your ways actually work! And the more we say "yes," the more we find we want to say "yes" in ways that are deeper and more encompassing. How mysterious and wonderful you are!

We are nervous, God, when we approach you with our needs. We feel we cannot come before you if we are not honest about ourselves.

For some of us, the flame and glow of serving has grown dim, as with Moses in the wilderness once the burning bush was extinguished. Some of us have lost our way in the deserts of our lives. Our enthusiasm for the beauties of life has hardened into simple plans for survival. God, help us overcome our feelings of resignation. Help us feel again what it is that we believe, see again what waits in our dreams, and dream again of what we can do for you. Rekindle in us the passion for new life. Breathe upon our glowing embers and ignite our flame. This Advent, free us to love again. Amen. (Luke 21:25–36)

Giver of gifts, we know we are not lacking in any spiritual gift, and yet we are not all on your journey of faith. Help us worry less about what's wrong with other people and focus more on being loving, hopeful, forgiving, and supportive. Let us remember all those who have died trying to bring mercy, healing, and faith to others: [list their names]. For their witness, we give you thanks. Amen.

In the time to come, O Mother, in times of confusion and needing, in the stumbling of doubts and fears, as our relationships stretch and test their bonds, be present with your caring arms. Comfort and nurture us into fullness. Out of you comes this life, and only with you does it continue. O birthing Spirit, move us now with your rhythms!

Assurance

God watches out over us when we are away from one another, protecting us, caring for us, guiding us. And if we stay faithful in our watching for God, we will see God's unexpected blessings all around us, as the shepherds did on that night long ago.

When we humble ourselves, God welcomes us. When we ask for help, God hears. God comforts the brokenhearted and guides those who have lost their way. God is with us.
    As the rain falls to water the earth, as seeds grow to nourishing grain, God's Word will not return to God empty or unfulfilled. It will not return until our longing for God is filled.

Benedictions

Humility

1 THESSALONIANS 3:9–13

One:	Go and make a new beginning.
Many:	We ask for humility and trust.
One:	Go and deepen your life in the Holy Spirit.
Many:	We ask that we may see the spirit of Jesus Christ around us.
One:	Go with the love of Jesus and the power of the Spirit.
Many:	So be it. This service is ended. Let our service begin.

Hope

PHIL. 1:3–11

One:	We have gathered in the name and spirit of Jesus Christ.
Many:	We have gathered as God's people, uniting our voices.
One:	Let us take, then, the promise of faith into the events of a new week.
Many:	Let us take, then, the compassion of Christ into the workings of our lives.
One:	Let us go as ministers of this church to serve God and love our neighbors with all the compassion and mercy we can muster.
Many:	Amen.

Appendix C

Resources for Special Days

Rosa Parks and World AIDS Day

December 1

On this day in 1955, Rosa Parks refused to move to the back of the bus and give up her seat to a white person. Her arrest was the spark that set the Montgomery bus boycott in motion.

Also on this day all those who have died or are living with AIDS and HIV, as well as their caregivers, are remembered as the search for a cure continues.

Prayer for Rosa Parks

God who sits, we have waited so long for your birth. We yearn to shed the night that threatens to overshadow us. We long with people of all generations to be sheltered in your presence. Today we remember Rosa Parks, who in 1955 gave birth to a movement for human rights by refusing to move to the back of the bus. Like her, we desire to be people of vision and strength, that we may know when to sit down and refuse to be moved by the immoral persuasion of racism, and that we may know when to stand up and be heard in the heroic fight against AIDS. O Light of the world, give us the vision to see that your warmth is needed, as well as your strength to carry it to those who are struggling to fend off the hollowing cold of despair. Amen.

Prayer for AIDS Day

God of Compassion, help us see what is going on around us and inside us. Help us focus today on the presence of AIDS in the world. Guide us in being sensitive to the needs of those who are afflicted—their families, partners, and caregivers. Let us remember those who are HIV-positive and struggling not to give up. Help them see each day as a new beginning, a new chance to grow closer to you. Help us not to fade like the sunset in a friend's eyes when times become difficult. Instead, let us watch for Christ's presence and for opportunities where we can be bearers of Christ's compassion. Let us be mindful that if we do not show our concern, Christ's love may not be felt. Help us realize that today is not a dress rehearsal for something that is coming. This is it! Amen.

Martin Luther King Jr. Sunday

Sunday nearest January 15

Service

Words of Preparation

"One day we shall win our freedom, but not only for ourselves. We shall so appeal to your heart and conscience that we shall win you in the process, and our victory will be a double victory." (Martin Luther King, Jr.)

After a prelude, the choir and congregation join in the processional hymn, "Lift Every Voice and Sing," by James Weldon and John Rosamond Johnson.

Call To Worship

One: Your love, Yahweh, reaches to heaven; your faithfulness to the skies.

Many: Your justice is like a mountain; your judgments like the deep. To all creation you give protection.

One:	Your people find refuge in the shelter of your wings.
Many:	They feast on the riches of your house; they drink from the stream of your delight.
One:	You are the source of life, and in your light we see light.
Many:	Continue your love to those who know you, doing justice to the upright in heart (based on Ps. 36:5–10).

A hymn is sung, followed by the reading of Isaiah 62:–4 and the anthem "Precious Lord, Take My Hand," by Thomas A. Dorsey.

Meditation

A READING FOR MARTIN

Reader 1:	Dear brother, what have we done to you?
Reader 2:	What have we done to your dream? Did we really know who you were?
Reader 1:	Did we want to know?
Reader 2:	Were you ready to be the hero for us?
Reader 1:	Were we ready to heed your call for freedom and justice? Are we ready now?
Reader 2:	You showed us how to be true to our faith by putting your own life on the line. You reminded us that we are here not to live long lives (although that has its place), but to carry the message of Jesus Christ to all people.
Reader 1:	You allowed yourself to be beaten and imprisoned, spat upon and threatened, until they finally murdered you. But your voice has not been stilled.

Reader 2: Your words continue to challenge us, to irritate our reasonable plans, to move us into places that we aren't sure we want to go.

Reader 1: You were a pastor and a leader, a seeker and a teacher, a husband and a father. You held up the Constitution and the Bible and challenged us to see the connections.

Reader 2: So often you were a step ahead of us, and we struggled to catch up to the fullness of your vision. From civil rights for African Americans, you encouraged us to see everyone's rights; from economic segregation, you tried to move us to see that institutionalized poverty trapped even more people of all cultures. And in the midst of it all, you showed us that change is possible, but only if we were willing to take a chance and speak out for justice.

Reader 1: You saw deeper than most of us and realized that justice involved more than just changing laws. It involved changing hearts.

Reader 2: Many years have passed since the Montgomery bus boycott of 1955. Over the next thirteen years, you marched and went to jail to desegregate lunch counters and washrooms. Your march on Washington in 1963 expressed the soul of a generation and led to the passage of the Civil Rights Act and the Voting Rights Act.

Reader 1: Wherever people were beaten down, you were there to lift them up.

Reader 2: While some pushed only for black power and black rights, you spoke of the need to continue to uphold human power and human rights.

Reader 1: We find it hard to believe that more than thirty years have passed since your death. What have we done

	since then? We have lost your vision and betrayed your dream. The struggle is far from over. Each day a little more is chipped away from the gains for which you died.
Reader 2:	If Martin were here today, would we be ready this time? And if he questioned our values and our bank accounts, how would we respond? What would Martin say of our support of governments for political and economic gains but not for gains in education and justice?
Reader 1:	But we have not gathered here today just to remember Martin Luther King Jr. We are here to remember his words and to find ways to keep his dream alive. Let us resolve to walk with Martin in the dream and build a better future.
Both Readers:	The word was justice. It was spoken. So it shall be spoken. So it shall be done. Amen.

Unison Prayer

Compassionate God, we pray for justice because your people are suffering the effects of greed, power, and racism in this world. We pray for healing, that we may recover from the effects of violence and deprivation in our lives. We pray for your good news, that we may find hope to dream again about the future. And we pray for peace, that we may all find joy in sitting together as brothers and sisters under fig trees and not being afraid (Micah 4:4). Amen.

Words of Assurance

Yahweh, ever faithful, sends justice to those who have been denied it, healing to those who are broken, good news to those eager to hear, and peace to our hearts and minds so that we may trust one another again and bear one another's burdens.

The closing hymn is sung: "Keep the Dream Alive," by Robert Manuel.

Benediction

May God grant us visions of truth, faith to witness in the midst of injustice, courage to endure, and the hope to carry us to the end. Go forth now as a people of justice. Amen.

Black History Month

February

Black History Month is a time of paying special tribute to the African American heritage and culture in the United States. The celebration began in 1926 as Negro History Week and is a time of remembering the past, acknowledging the present, and preparing for the future.

On the Sundays of the month, churches can focus on the black church—its West African roots, its development alongside the white church structure, and its impact on black history. Black music can be celebrated, with special attention paid to the variety of music in the black church: spirituals, gospel, and metered hymns. Music and other art forms can be looked at as expressions of worship, art, and protest. Your church may choose to sponsor a black poetry reading or to display tapestries and paintings by black artists on the walls of the sanctuary. Other themes can involve the black family and the development of community resources.

Include preachers and interfaith choirs in your worship service, and invite guests to lead special forums on various topics and community needs. Sponsor a film festival featuring videos on the civil rights movement and other historical themes, or the films of black directors such as Robert Townsend and Spike Lee. Invite black community leaders to talk about their work. Put inserts into your Sunday program that tell about historic events and the lives of black leaders like Carter Godwin Wood-son, Mary McLeod Bethune, W. E. B. DuBois, Shirley Chisholm, George Washington Carver, and June Jordan. Meet as a congregation to discuss your church's effectiveness in welcoming, affirming, and involving people of all races.

Because people of African descent have been in the United States for over 350 years, congregations should not attempt to cover all aspects of black history within the month. Rather, some observances should occur throughout the year. The black national anthem, "Lift Every Voice and Sing," by James Weldon and John Rosamond Johnson, is an important part of each year's celebration.

Central America Sunday

Sunday before March 24

A Service for Central America Sunday

"Some want to keep a gospel so disembodied that it doesn't get involved at all in the world it must save. Christ is now in history.... Christ is now bringing about the new heavens and the new earth" (Archbishop Oscar Romero).

CALL TO WORSHIP

One:	In truth, I tell you, a grain of wheat remains a solitary grain unless it falls into the earth and dies. But if it dies, it bears a rich harvest. The people who love themselves are lost. Today we remember those who bear the message of Christ in Central America.
Many:	They live in torn countries and try to bring hope to the people. They do it not for their own glory, but for God's. They see the need, and their hearts are moved. And although they know that they might be killed, as others have been killed before them, they still serve. They feel they can do no less.
One:	Jesus says, "Whoever would serve me, must follow me. Where I am, my servants will be. Whoever serves me will be honored by God. Now my soul is in turmoil, and what am I to say? God, save me from this hour? No. It was for this that I came to this hour."
Many:	They work and live with the poor, doing what they can to relieve the misery and terror of daily life. Christ hears the cry of the poor!

One:	Blessed be Jesus the Christ! God will lift up every crushed spirit, and in God's loving arms every fear will be calmed!
Many:	We know that those who die in Christ's name do not die in vain. They go before us to prepare a place. But they are also with us, helping us to hear the depth of Christ's challenge, daring us to embody God's Word with our lives, showing us how to hope when the world around us becomes a hell.

Litany of Commitment

One:	How can we offer God thanks for our lives if we do not go to those whose hearts are heavy and whose lives are broken, offering them the faith that we bear in Christ's name? The harvest is plentiful. The laborers are few. Come with me into the fields.
Many:	We remember today the witness of Oscar Romero, Archbishop of El Salvador, who said that what was spoken in church must find action in our lives. He continued to preach peace to all sides of the warring factions even after numerous death threats. Then he was gunned down in the midst of celebrating Holy Communion.
One:	Our arms will grow weary and our shoes will wear thin, but we will follow our God throughout the world.
Many:	We believe in history. The world is not a roll of dice. A new world has begun with Christ! Beyond the difficulties of our existence lives an eternal alleluia! We know that God dries the tears of the oppressed and comforts those in sorrow. Christ, teach us to give voice to this new life in the world.

One:	May we, like Oscar Romero, speak out against injustice. May we object with our lives to murder, to torture, and to terror that picks away at the hopes of people. And let us invite others to stand beside us.
All:	May Almighty God bless us: God who created us, Jesus who saves us, and the Spirit who sets us free! Amen.

Responsive Reading: Time to Repair

One:	Brothers and sisters, it is time again to repair the church.
Many:	This does not mean we must repair the buildings made of wood and stone, but rather the church that lives inside us.
One:	We share a simple vision of great worth. Over the centuries, we've constructed rituals and formulas of words to protect and preserve this treasure. But rituals lose the poignancy of their symbolism, words change their meanings, and often we are uncertain about which way to turn when technology raises questions that have never been asked.
Many:	Let us return to a simple faith in which we speak about God in the words that are in our hearts and we express our faith through the experiences of our lives.
One:	We think there are many differences between Congregationalists and Baptists, Methodists and Episcopalians. We feel there are even greater differences between Protestants and Roman Catholics, between the Greek and Russian Orthodox. But these differences are not important, because we all seek the same God.

Many:	There are as many differences within this congregation as there are among denominations, yet we all worship together.
One:	We rebuild the church not by tearing down hollow structures that have lost their meaning. We rebuild by starting with the foundation of our faith.
Many:	We rebuild by listening for God's voice in our lives:
One:	We rebuild by setting aside what distracts us from following God more closely.
Many:	We rebuild by humbling ourselves so that we live without pre-tense, without illusion, without any need to make something of ourselves; for we serve God, not ourselves.
One:	We rebuild by sharing our struggles with one another and by listening for God's message in others' words. By learning from one another, we strengthen the community of faith.
Many:	We rebuild by welcoming those marginalized by poverty, illness, or wealth.
Many:	Saint Francis calls us to live a simple life, to celebrate the goodness of all creation;
Many:	To sing with the songs of the birds, dance with the trees in the wind, and dream with the movement of the stars.

Prayer

One:	Personal God, you live all around us. Holy is your name.
Many:	May your world come and your will be done on earth.

One:	Give us today the things we need, and forgive us when we turn away from you.
Many:	Help us forgive those who hurt us.
One:	Help us not to be led away by temptation but to be delivered from questionable activities.
Many:	For yours is the way of life we desire, the power to make it happen, and the wisdom that lasts forever.
All:	Amen.

Unison Prayer

Religion sometimes gets in the way of our faith, O God of all creation. We confess that we hide behind church forms for assurance when we are confused, that we too often let Sunday worship take the place of our faith. Instead of praying each day on our own, we rely on the church's prayers on Sunday. Instead of dealing with the responsibilities our participation in communion gives us, we let the Sunday worship service be the extent of our ministry. Instead of leaving here to share the good news with the world, we let our pastors shoulder this responsibility. We have become like hollow buildings, well designed and beautiful but empty inside. Each new problem that drops into our lives echoes the depth of our loneliness.

Help us, O God, to feel again your movement in our lives. Help us share again with others and see again what your hope means to them. Help us always to live faithfully and simply, that nothing may get in the way of serving you. Help us always to love one another that our differences will not build up new walls of separation. Help us celebrate the sacredness of every living thing and the presence of your Spirit in every single person, that we may be a true and enduring community. Amen.

APPENDIX D

Liturgical, Cultural, and Historical Dates

Day by Day

As your church grows in its understanding of diversity, add new dates to this list.

November

Advent begins on the fourth Sunday before December 25, the Sunday nearest November 30.

27   Earliest date for the start of Advent; Feast Day of Saint James; Feast Day of Saint Paladius; Harvey Milk dies, 1978

28   Berry Gordy Jr. (founder of Motown Records) born, 1929

29   C. S. Lewis born, 1898; Dorothy Day dies, 1980

30   Feast Day of Saint Andrew the apostle; Shirley Chisholm born, 1924; Etty Hillesum dies in Auschwitz, 1943

December

Advent continues, comprising the four Sundays before December 25. Hanukkah (the Jewish Feast Day of Lights) occurs in November/December, beginning on the twenty-fifth day of Kislev. In 167 B.C.E., Judas Maccabee led a small group of soldiers against the larger army of the Syrian king Antiochus because the Syrians had defiled the

Temple in Jerusalem. The Jews drove the Syrians out of the Temple and rededicated it with holy oil that miraculously lasted eight days. This is the event celebrated during the eight days of Hanukkah.

1   World AIDS Day; Rosa Parks sits in the front of the bus, 1955; Japanese Festival of the Water (Spirit)

2   Latest date for the start of Advent; four churchwomen murdered in El Salvador, 1980

3   Feast Day of Saint Francis Xavier (1506–52)

4   Feast Day of Clement of Alexandria; Rainer Maria Rilke born, 1875; Cesar Chavez jailed twenty days (lettuce boycott)

5   Feast Day of Crispina, African woman martyred at Thebaste in 304 CE; Montgomery bus boycott began, 1955

6   Feast Day of Saint Nicholas (died 342 CE, in Turkey); Agnes Moorhead born, 1900

7   Feast Day of Saint Ambrose (patron saint of domestic animals, died 397 CE); Willa Cather born, 1873

8   Feast Day of Immaculate Conception of Mary; Diego Rivera born, 1886; Martin Luther King Jr. receives the Nobel Peace Prize, 1964

9   John Milton born, 1608; New York City Gay Men's Chorus performs at Carnegie Hall, 1984

10   International Human Rights Day; Thomas Gallaudet born, 1787; Red Cloud (Sioux) dies, 1909

11   Lars Skrefsrud, 1910; Aleksandr Solzhenitsyn born, 1918

12   Feast Day of Our Lady of Guadalupe (Mexico); Joseph Rainey, first African American U.S. congressman sworn into Congress, 1870

13   Saint Lucia's Day (Swedish feast of lights); annual meteor shower

14	Feast Day of John of the Cross (died 1591); Feast Day of Teresa of Avila (died 1582); Drestan, Abbot of Deer (ca. 600, Scotland)
15	Feast Day of Saint Eleutherius (Byzantine); Jose Marti born, 1853; Chief Sitting Bull (Hunkpapa Sioux) dies, 1890
16	Las Posadas begins; O Sapientia (Scotland); Ludwig van Beethoven born, 1770; Ozone Treaty signed, 1988
17	Feast Day of Saint Ignatius (martyred in Antioch, ca. 110 CE); the Wright brothers' first flight, 1903
18	Slavery abolished (13th Amendment), 1865; Dorothy Sayers remembered (1893–1957); Operation PUSH founded, 1971
19	Feast Day of Saint Boniface (Byzantine)
20	Sacajawea remembered (Shoshoni guide and peacemaker, 1786–1812)
21	Winter of the hundred slain, 1866; Henrietta Szold born, 1860; Montgomery buses integrated, 1956
22	Winter solstice (Northern Hemisphere); annual meteor shower
23	Juan Ramon Jimenez (Spanish poet) born, 1881; Chico Mendes (Brazil) killed, 1988
24	Las Posadas ends; Christmas Eve; John Muir dies, 1914
25	Christmas Day; beginning of the twelve days of Christmas; Quentin Crisp born, 1908
26	Kwanzaa begins; Boxing Day; Feast Day of Saint Stephen the martyr; Jean Toomer born, 1894
27	Second day of Kwanzaa; Feast Day of Saint John (apostle and evangelist)

28   Holy Innocents Day; third day of Kwanzaa; Charles Wesley remembered (1708–1788)

29   Fourth day of Kwanzaa; Feast Day of Saint Thomas Becket; battle of Wounded Knee, 1890; Rainer Maria Rilke dies, 1926

30   Fifth day of Kwanzaa; Feast of the Holy Family; John Howard Yoder dies, 1997

31   Watch Night; sixth day of Kwanzaa; John Wyclif dies (1324–1384)

January

Las Pastores is observed in early January. Martin Luther King Jr. Sunday is observed on the Sunday nearest January 15.

The baptism of Jesus is commemorated on the first Sunday after January 6. The Season after Epiphany begins on January 7 and continues until Ash Wednesday (the earliest date of Ash Wednesday is February 6, the latest is March 10). Chinese New Year occurs between January 10 and February 19. The Jewish holiday of Tu B'shvat, an agricultural holiday that looks forward to the spring planting, is observed on the fifteenth day of Shvat (usually January).

1   Feast of the Circumcision and Naming of Jesus; New Year's Day; World Day of Prayer for Peace; seventh and last day of Kwanzaa; Shogatsu Day of Purification (Japan); Day of the Covenant (Church of South India); Emancipation Proclamation issued, 1865

2   Feast Day of Saints Basil and Gregory of Nazianzus

3   J. R. R. Tolkien born, 1892; Simone Weil born, 1909; first lesbian center in the United States opens (New York City), 1971

4   Annual meteor shower; earth nearest the sun; Louis Braille born, 1809

5	Twelfth Night; Alvin Ailey born, 1931; George Washington Carver dies, 1943
6	Feast of the Epiphany (Christ to the Gentiles); Feast of the Three Magi; Dance Theater of Harlem founded, 1971
7	Zora Neale Hurston born, 1891; DDT banned, 1971
8	Galileo dies, 1642; A. J. Muste born, 1885; Stephen Hawking born, 1942
9	Simone de Beauvoir born, 1908; Joan Baez born, 1941
10	George Washington Carver born, 1886; Robinson Jeffers born, 1887
11	Aldo Leopold (founder of Wilderness Society) born, 1887
12	Southern Christian Leadership Conference founded, 1957; Lorraine Hansberry dies, 1965
13	George Fox dies, 1691; Lawrence Wilder became first African American governor, 1990
14	Harriet Tubman remembered (1821–1913); Albert Schweitzer born, 1875; Chief Joseph (Nez Perce) dies, 1879; Julian Bond born, 1940
15	Martin Luther King Jr. born, 1929
16	Susan Sontag born, 1933
17	Whale migrations along the West Coast; Muhammad Ali born, 1942
18	Week of Christian prayer begins (January 18–25); Feast of the Confession of Saint Peter; A. A. Milne born, 1882
19	John Harold Johnson (publisher of Ebony) born, 1918
20	Richard Le Gallienne born, 1866
21	Huddie "Leadbelly" Ledbetter born, 1885
22	August Strindberg born, 1849

23 E Stendhal born, 1783; 24th Amendment ratified (abolishing the poll tax), 1964

24 Edith Wharton born, 1862; Ernesto Cardenal born, 1925; George Cukor dies, 1985

25 Feast of the Conversion of Saint Paul; Robert Burns born, 1759

26 Republic Day (Church of South India); Eugene Sue born, 1804; Angela Davis born, 1928

27 Wolfgang Amadeus Mozart born, 1756; Lewis Carroll born, 1832

28 Endangered Species Law enacted, 1973

29 Anton Chekhov born, 1860

30 Holiday of the Three Hierarchs (Greek Orthodox); Mohandas Gandhi killed, 1948

31 Jackie Robinson born, 1914; Thomas Merton born, 1915

February

February is designated as Black History Month in the United States. Islamic people also commemorate Mohammed's Ascension during February. Chinese New Year occurs between January 10 and February 19. Hindu people observe Mahashivarathi during February. The Jewish Feast of Purim is celebrated on the thirteenth day of Adar (February to March). It is a remembrance of Queen Esther, who saved the Jewish people from death at the hands of her husband King Ahasuerus of Persia. Purim is a time of celebration and silliness.

Lent usually begins in February. The first day of Lent, Ash Wednesday, occurs on the seventh Wednesday before Easter. (The earliest date is February 6; the latest is March 10.) The Sunday before Ash Wednesday (the last Sunday after Epiphany) is Transfiguration Sunday (although it is observed on August 6 by Catholics and Episcopalians).

Liturgical, Cultural and Historical Dates 161

1   S. Brigit remembered; Langston Hughes born, 1902; Greensboro Woolworth lunch counter sit-in, 1960

2   Presentation of Jesus in the Temple; Candlemas Day; Groundhog Day

3   Elizabeth Blackwell (first woman doctor) remembered, 1821; Gertrude Stein born, 1874; Simone Weil born, 1909

4   Winter is half over; Rosa Parks born, 1913; Betty Friedan born, 1921; Liberace dies, 1987

5   Henry Aaron born, 1934

6   Earliest date for Ash Wednesday and the beginning of Lent; Bob Marley (Jamaica) born, 1945

7   Eubie Blake born, 1883; Carter Woodson began Negro History Week in 1926

8   Martin Buber born, 1878; Elizabeth Bishop born, 1911

9   Alice Walker born, 1944

10   Boris Pasternak born, 1890; Leontyne Price born, 1927; Bill Sherwood dies, 1990

11   Thomas Edison born, 1847; Nelson Mandela (South Africa) freed, 1990

12   Abraham Lincoln born, 1809; NAACP founded, 1909

13   Georges Simenon born, 1903; SCLC founded, 1957

14   Feast Day of Saint Valentine (third-century priest in Rome); Frederick Douglass born, 1817

15   Buddha born, 563 BCE; Susan B. Anthony born, 1820; A. N. Whitehead born, 1862

16   Octave Mirbeau born, 1850

17   Geronimo (Apache) dies, 1909

18   Martin Luther dies, 1546; Toni Morrison born, 1931; Audre Lorde born, 1934

19   Nicolaus Copernicus born, 1473; Japanese American Day of Remembrance (recalling the internment camps) established, 1978

20   Bill Tilden born, 1893; Frederick Douglass dies, 1895; Sidney Poitier born, 1927

21   Peter Damien remembered (1844–1888, Molokai, Hawaii); W. H. Auden born, 1907; Barbara Jordan born, 1936; Campaign for Nuclear Disarmament founded, 1948; Malcolm X assassinated, 1965

22   George Washington born, 1732; Edna St. Vincent Millay born, 1892; Ishmael Reed born, 1938

23   George Frideric Handel born, 1685; W. E. B. DuBois born, 1868; supernova, 1987

24   Wilhelm Grimm born, 1786

25   Anthony Burgess born, 1917

26   Victor Hugo born, 1802

27   Marian Anderson born, 1902; John Steinbeck born, 1902; Christian Haren dies, 1996

28   Michel de Montaigne born, 1533; Phyllis Wheatley (poet) dies, 1784

29   Hattie McDaniel became the first African American to receive an Academy Award, 1940

March

March is designated as Women's History Month in the United States. The third week of March is designated as Central America Week. The Jewish Feast of Purim (Esther) is celebrated on the thirteenth day of Adar (February to March). Passover (Pesac, Feast of Unleavened Bread) is observed on the fourteenth to twenty-first days of Nisan (March to April). Originally a spring festival, it was paired with the Feast of Unleavened Bread to include the symbolism of the tenth plague sent by God upon the Egyptians, the salvation of the firstborn Jewish children, and Jewish liberation from Egyptian slavery.

Lent sometimes begins in March. The first day of Lent, Ash Wednesday, occurs on the seventh Wednesday before Easter. (The earliest date is February 6; the latest is March 10.) The Sunday before Ash Wednesday (the last Sunday after Epiphany) is Transfiguration Sunday (although it is observed on August 6 by Catholics and Episcopalians). Easter may also occur during March. (The earliest date is March 23; the latest is April 25.) The fifty days of Eastertide begin on Easter Sunday and end on Pentecost Day.

1	George Herbert remembered (1593–1633); Yellowstone National Park founded, 1872; Ralph Ellison born, 1914; Merlie Evers-Williams born, 1933
2	Scholem Aleichem born, 1859; William Stringfellow dies, 1985
3	Doll Festival (Japan); Edmund Waller born, 1606
4	Antonio Vivaldi born, 1678; Jane Goodall born, 1934
5	Isidora (fifth-century "fool for Christ") born; Leontine Kelly (African American bishop) born, 1920
6	Michelangelo born, 1475; Elizabeth Barrett Browning born, 1806; Dred Scott decision 1857; Gabriel Garcia Marquez born, 1928
7	Saint Perpetua and companions martyred (Carthage), 202 CE
8	International Women's Day
9	Vita Sackville-West born, 1892; Paula Marshall born, 1929
10	Latest date for Ash Wednesday; Tibet Freedom Day; Angela Saavedra (Spanish poet) remembered, 1791; Harriet Tubman dies, 1913

11	Johnny Appleseed Day; Ralph Abernathy born, 1926
12	Sandhill Crane Watch Day (Nebraska); Jack Kerouac born, 1922; Edward Albee born, 1928
13	Gutenberg Bible published, 1462; Kofi Awoonor born, 1935
14	Albert Einstein born, 1879
15	Ides of March; Julius Caesar dies, 44 BCE
16	Arrival of long-billed curlews in Oregon; My Lai Massacre in Vietnam, 1968
17	Saint Patrick's Day; Nat King Cole born, 1919
18	Feast Day of Mechtild of Magdeburg (1209–1282); Andrew Young born, 1932; Unita Blackwell born, 1935
19	Swallows return to Capistrano; Lao Tzu remembered, 550 BCE; Ornette Coleman born, 1930
20	Spring equinox (Northern Hemisphere); Patsy Takemoto Mink (Hawaii) elected to U.S. House of Representatives, 1964
21	J. S. Bach born, 1685; Selma-to-Montgomery march starts, 1965
22	O. E. Rolvaag born, 1876; Marcel Marceau born, 1923; Equal Rights Amendment passed, 1972
23	Earliest date for Easter; World Meteorological Day; Akira Kurosawa born, 1910
24	Archbishop Oscar Romero (El Salvador) killed, 1980; ACT UP's first demonstration, 1987
25	Feast of the Annunciation to Mary; Flannery O'Connor born, 1925; Aretha Franklin born, 1942
26	Robert Frost born, 1874; Anne Frank killed at Bergen-Belsen, 1945

27   Alice Herz born, 1867; Shusaku Endo born, 1923

28   Three Mile Island meltdown, 1979; Mario Vargas Llosa born, 1936

29   Howard Lindsay born, 1889; Pearl Bailey born, 1918

30   Spring Corn Dance (American Indian); Vincent van Gogh born, 1863; African American suffrage, 1870

31   John Donne dies, 1631; Cesar Chavez born, 1927 April

April

The month of April includes part of Eastertide, which encompasses the fifty days between Easter and Pentecost, beginning March 23 to April 25 and ending May 11 to June 13. The Aztec Spring Festival, the Cherry Blossom Festival, and Spring Planting are celebrated during April. Yom Hashoah, Holocaust Remembrance Day, is observed on the twenty-sixth day of Nisan (March to April).

1   Nazi Germany began persecution of Jews, 1933; Charles Drew (hematologist) dies, 1950

2   James Joyce born, 1882

3   Septima Poinsetta Clark born, 1898; Carter G. Woodson dies, 1950; Martin Luther King Jr.'s "Mountaintop" speech delivered, 1968

4   Maya Angelou born, 1928; Martin Luther King Jr. assassinated (Memphis), 1968

5   Booker T. Washington born, 1856; Colin Powell born, 1937

6   North Pole reached, 1909; Bob Marley born, 1945

7   World Health Day; Billie Holiday born, 1915

8   Benjamin Lindner killed by Contras (Nicaragua), 1986

9	Paul Robeson born, 1898; W. B. Yeats dies, 1939; Dietrich Bonhoeffer killed by Nazis, 1945; Ryan White dies of AIDS at the age of eighteen, 1990; 65,000 March for Equal Rights, 1989
10	Mechtild of Hackenborn remembered; Teilhard de Chardin born, 1881; Frida Kahlo born, 1910; Arthur Ashe born, 1943; Jackie Robinson joins the Dodgers, 1947; first Arbor Day held in Nebraska (date varies by location)
11	Glenway Wescott born, 1901
12	Andrew Young born, 1932
13	Eudora Welty born, 1909
14	Abraham Lincoln killed, 1865; Katherine Dunham (choreographer) born, 1910
15	Titanic sinks, 1912
16	Charlie Chaplin born, 1889; Martin Luther King Jr.'s letter from the Birmingham jail written, 1963
17	Isak Dinesen born, 1885
18	Richard Harding Davis born, 1864
19	Jose Echegaray born, 1832; Dick Sargent born, 1930
20	Chief Pontiac (Ottawa), dies, 1769; Herman Bang born, 1857
21	Annual meteor shower; John Muir born, 1838; Bergen-Belsen liberated, 1945
22	Earth Day instituted, 1970
23	Toyohiko Kagawa (Japan); William Shakespeare born, 1564; UN Law of the Sea passed, 1982
24	World Children's Day; Dorothy Uhnak born, 1930
25	Latest date for Easter; Feast Day of Saint Mark the evangelist (Church of South India); Ella Fitzgerald born, 1918

26	John Audubon born, 1785; Bishop Juan Gerardi (Guatemala) killed, 1998
27	Coretta Scott King born, 1927
28	Tulip Festival (Holland)
29	Saint Catherine of Sienna dies, 1380; Duke Ellington born, 1899; Katherine Forrest born, 1939; American Indian Movement begins, 1968
30	Countee Cullen born, 1903; Annie Dillard born, 1945; Vietnam War ends, 1975

May

May is designated as Asian-Pacific Heritage Month. Mother's Day, which began as a protest against war, is celebrated on the second Sunday of May. Peace Sunday is often celebrated in May, and Memorial Day is observed on the Sunday before May 30. Ascension Day, often during May, is observed forty days after Easter. Ascension Sunday (May 4–June 6) is the sixth Sunday after Easter. The seventh Sunday after Easter (May 11 June 13) is Pentecost Day. The season of Pentecost begins on Pentecost Day and ends November 26 to December 2. The eighth Sunday after Easter (May 18 June 20) is Trinity Sunday. Shavuot, the Jewish Pentecost (Feast Day of Weeks), is observed fifty days after Passover, in May or June. It began as a celebration of the first fruits of the wheat harvest; later a celebration of the giving of the Torah was added.

1	May Day (the halfway point between spring equinox and summer solstice); Feast Day of Saint Joseph the worker
2	Leonardo da Vinci remembered (1452–1519)
3	Dia de la Cruz; Golda Meir born, 1898; U.S. Bishops Peace Pastoral issued, 1983
4	Feast Day of Saint Pelagia of Tarsus (martyr, Eastern Orthodox Church)

5	Cinco de Mayo (Mexico); Soren Kierkegaard born, 1813; Chief Kickingbird (Kiowa) dies, 1875
6	Saint George's Day; Feast Day of John the apostle (Church of South India); Maria Montessori born, 1870
7	Johannes Brahms born, 1833; Rabindranath Tagore born, 1862
8	Julian of Norwich remembered (1342–after 1416); Peter Maurin born, 1876; Gary Snyder born, 1930
9	Daniel Berrigan born, 1921
10	NAACP incorporated, 1910; Judith Jamison born, 1943
11	Earliest date for Day of Pentecost
12	Florence Nightingale born, 1820; H. Rap Brown becomes chair of the SNCC, 1967
13	Stevie Wonder born, 1950
14	Mochuda of Lismore remembered (Irish Church), 637 CD.
15	Feast Day of Saints Isidore and Maria (patron saints of farm workers); International Conscientious Objectors' Day
16	Victoria Day (Canada); Native American Day; Joan of Arc born, 1412
17	Syttende Mai (holiday); Supreme Court desegregation ruling, 1954
18	Earliest date for Trinity Sunday; Mary McLeod Bethune dies, 1955
19	Malcolm X born, 1925
20	Bread for the World instituted, 1974
21	Lag B'omer (holiday); Fats Waller born, 1904; Raymond Burr born, 1917

22	Benjamin Davis Jr. becomes first African American general in U.S. Air Force, 1959; Langston Hughes dies, 1967; Harvey Milk born, 1930
23	Cherokee Nation forced to vacate all land east of the Mississippi River (the "Trail of Tears"), 1839
24	Feast Day of Saints Cyril and Methodius (missionaries to Czechoslovakia); Duke Ellington dies, 1974
25	Miles Davis born, 1926
26	Charles Anderson (Kentucky) born, 1907
27	Rachel Carson (environmentalist) born, 1903
28	Sierra Club founded, 1892
29	U.S. Navy concludes that homosexuals in the military do not create a security risk, 1957
30	Memorial Day (U.S.) began when Southern women honored the graves of both sides after the Civil War battle of Shiloh
31	Walt Whitman remembered (1819–1892); G. K. Chesterton born, 1874; Gloria Molina born, 1948

June

June is designated as Lesbian and Gay History Month, and the last Sunday of the month is Gay/Lesbian Pride Sunday. The third Sunday in June is Father's Day. Ascension Day, sometimes during June, is observed forty days after Easter. Ascension Sunday (May 4–June 6) is the sixth Sunday after Easter. The seventh Sunday after Easter (May 11 June 13) is Pentecost Day. The season of Pentecost begins on Pentecost Day and ends November 26 to December 2. The eighth Sunday after Easter (May 18 June 20) is Trinity Sunday. Shavuot, the Jewish Pentecost (Feast Day of Weeks), is observed fifty days after Passover, in May or June.

Liturgical, Cultural and Historical Dates

1. Slavery begins in Virginia, 1619; Harriet Tubman born, 1826; Father Jacques Marquette born, 1637

2. Rice Harvest Festival (Japan); Native American citizenship, 1924

3. Feast Day of Lucillian and companions (martyrs, Eastern Orthodox Church); Pope John XXIII dies, 1963

4. International Day of Innocent Children, victims of aggression

5. World Environmental Day (instituted 1972); James Meredith's "March against Fear," 1966

6. Marian Edelman born, 1939; Robert Kennedy killed, 1968

7. Chief Seattle (Suquamish) dies, 1866; Gwendolyn Brooks born, 1917; Nikki Giovanni born, 1943

8. Mohammed dies, 632 CE; Aedh of Terryglass (Ireland) dies, 842 CE

9. Columba of Iona dies, 597 CE

10. Feast Day of the Sacred Heart of Jesus; founding of Alcoholics Anonymous, 1935

11. Feast Day of Barnabas the Apostle (Church of South India); G. M. Hopkins born, 1844

12. Djuna Barnes born, 1892; Barbara Harris (Episcopal bishop) born, 1930; Medgar Evers dies, 1963

13. Latest date for Pentecost Day; Thurgood Marshall appointed to U.S. Supreme Court, 1967

14. William Gray (African American) elected House Democratic Whip, 1989

15. Magna Carta, 1215

Liturgical, Cultural and Historical Dates 171

16 Soweto (South Africa) Massacre, 1976; Spelman College opens, 1881

17 Linda Chavez born, 1947; Stokely Carmichael calls for the Black Power movement, 1966

18 Unita Blackwell (first woman African American mayor in Mississippi) born, 1933

19 King James I (England, authorized the K.J.V. Bible) born, 1566; Juneteenth, slaves in Texas find out about the Emancipation Proclamation signed on January 1 (Black Emancipation Day), 1865

20 Latest date for Trinity Sunday; Midsummer's Eve

21 Summer begins (Northern Hemisphere; first full day)

22 Joe Lewis becomes the heavyweight boxing champion, 1937

23 Willie Mae Ford (gospel singer) born, 1904; Wilma Rudolph born, 1940

24 Feast Day of John the Baptist (Church of South India); Henry Ward Beecher born, 1813

25 Native American Day; battle of Little Big Horn, 1876

26 National University of El Salvador attacked by the army (26 killed), 1980

27 Emma Goldman born, 1869; Paul Dunbar (poet) born, 1872; Helen Keller born, 1880

28 Gay/Lesbian Pride Day; John Wesley remembered (1703–1791); Stonewall rebellion, 1969

29 Feast Day of Peter the apostle (Church of South India); Anne Frank born, 1929

30 Czeslaw Milosz born, 1911

July

1	Canada Day; John Bunyan born, 1629; Charles Laughton born, 1899; Benjamin Davis Sr. (first African American Army general) born, 1877
2	Thomas Cranmer remembered (1489–1556); Aldo Leopold born, 1907; Thurgood Marshall born, 1908; Medgar Evers born, 1925; Civil Rights Act passed, 1964
3	Chief Little Crow (Sioux) dies, 1863; Jackie Robinson inducted into the baseball Hall of Fame, 1962
4	U.S. Independence Day
5	Earth farthest from the sun
6	Jan Hus born, 1369, dies, 1415; Pablo Neruda born, 1904
7	Satchel Paige born, 1904
8	Dorothy Thompson (journalist) born, 1894; Alice Faye Wattleton born, 1943
9	June Jordan born, 1936
10	John Calvin remembered (1509–1564); Marcel Proust born, 1871
11	World Population Day
12	Henry David Thoreau born, 1817; Bill Cosby born, 1937
13	Synaxis of the archangel Gabriel (Eastern Orthodox Church)
14	Kateri Tekakwitha (Mohawk) born, 1656; Bastille Day, 1880; Isaac Bashevis Singer born, 1904
15	Feast Day of Saint Swithun of Winchester (Scottish Church, 862 CE); Rembrandt born, 1606
16	Feast Day of Scotha of Clonmore (Ireland); Katherine Ortega born, 1934; first A-Bomb detonated, 1945

17	Port Chicago ammunition explosion kills over two hundred African Americans, 1944
18	Nelson Mandela born, 1918
19	Feast Day of Saint Vincent de Paul; First women's rights conference, 1848; Temple Beth Chayim Chadashim becomes first U.S. Gay and Lesbian synagogue, 1974; Mark Wellman begins climbing El Capitan in Yosemite, 1989
20	Geneva Convention (peace agreement on Korea and Indochina), 1954
21	Feast Day of Saint Simeon (Eastern Orthodox Church)
22	Feast Day of Mary Magdalene (Church of South India); Gregor Mendel born, 1822
23	Fourteenth Amendment ratified, granting citizenship to all African Americans, 1868
24	Simon Bolivar remembered (1783–1830); Signing of Peace Treaty by Chief Pontiac, 1766
25	Feast Day of James the Apostle (Church of South India)
26	Carl Jung born, 1875; Americans with Disabilities Act signed into law, 1990
27	Annual meteor shower (through July 29)
28	Johann Sebastian Bach dies, 1750; Judy Grahn born, 1940
29	Dag Hammarskjold born, 1905
30	James Varick becomes the first bishop of the African Methodist Episcopal Zion Church, 1822
31	Feast Day of Saint Ignatius Loyola; Bartholome de las Casas dies, 1506; Whitney Young Jr. born, 1921

August

World Peace Day is observed on the First Sunday in August. In early August, American Indians hold intertribal celebrations.

1	Lammas Day (the midway point between summer solstice and autumn equinox)
	192 Calendar of the Church Year
2	James Baldwin born, 1924
3	Flannery O'Connor dies, 1964; Georgia police arrest Michael Hardwick for sodomy, 1982
4	The bodies of three civil rights workers are found outside Philadelphia, Mississippi, 1964
5	James Cone (theologian) born, 1938; Vitto Russo (journalist) dies, 1990
6	Feast of the Transfiguration of Christ (Catholic, Episcopal, and Church of South India); Hiroshima bombing, 1945; Voting Rights Act signed, 1965; Minnesota removes transgender discrimination, 1993
7	Ralph Bunche born, 1904; first photo of earth from Explorer VI, 1969
8	Executive order requiring equal employment opportunities in all federal agencies, 1969
9	F. Jaegerstetter dies, 1943; Nagasaki bombing, 1945; Adoniram Judson born, 1788
10	Saint Laurence dies, 258 CE (martyr, Scottish Church)
11	Clare of Assisi dies, 1253; John Rosamond Johnson (composer of the Black National Anthem, "Lift Every Voice and Sing") born, 1873
12	Annual meteor shower; Radclyffe Hall born, 1880

13	Feast Day of Saint Maximus, confessor (Eastern Orthodox Church)
14	S. Max Kolbe dies at Auschwitz; Social Security Act ratified, 1935
15	Feast Day of the Assumption of Mary; Independence Day (Church of South India); Oscar Romero born, 1917
16	Wyatt Tee Walker (SCLS director) born, 1929
17	Marcus Garvey born, 1887
18	Confucius born, 551 BC; James Meredith graduates from the University of Mississippi, 1963
19	Ralph Bunche named undersecretary of the United Nations, 1954
20	Fallen Timbers Massacre, 1794; Paul Tillich born, 1886; Bernard of Clairvaux born (1090–1153)
21	Sionach of Clonard dies, 588 CE (Irish Church); Count Basie born, 1904
22	Nat Turner begins a slave revolt in Virginia, 1831
23	Feast Day of Saints Luppus and Irenaeus (martyrs, Eastern Orthodox Church); Nina Simone born, 1933
24	Jorge Luis Borges born, 1899; Marlee Matlin born, 1965
25	Leonard Bernstein born, 1925; Althea Gibson born, 1927
26	19th Amendment (women's suffrage), 1920 (Women's Equality Day)
27	Mother Teresa born, 1910; W. E. B. Du Bois dies, 1963
28	Elizabeth Seton born, 1774; Leo Tolstoy, born, 1828; Martin Luther King's "I Have a Dream" speech (Washington D.C.), 1963; first Gay Games (San Francisco), 1982

29	Beheading of John the Baptist; Simone Weil dies, 1943
30	Fiachra of Breuil dies, 650 CE (Irish Church)
31	Feast Day of Aidan of Lindisfarne; Cherokee national holidays September

September

The period from September 15 to October 15 is designated as Hispanic Heritage Month. The first Monday in September is Labor Day. Churches also observe Homecoming Sunday and Christian Education Sunday during September.

Several Jewish holidays occur during the month of Tishri (September to October). Rosh Hashanah (New Year) is the first day of Tishri. Yom Kippur (Day of Atonement) is on the tenth; it is observed by fasting and mourning, admitting mistakes, and asking forgiveness. In ancient times, the observance was concluded by transferring the people's sins onto a scapegoat, which was released in the desert. Sukkoth (Feast of the Tabernacles), is observed on the fifteenth to twenty-second days of Tishri. Initially it was a ceremony of gratitude toward God that concluded the gathering of the crops. Over time, the meaning of the tents put up for the celebration came to include gratitude to God for the exodus which led them out of slavery and into freedom in the desert. Simchat Torah is observed on the twenty-third day of Tishri. It marks when one year's reading of the Torah ends and a new one begins.

1	Greek New Year's Day
2	Feast Day of John the Faster (sixth-century patriarch of Constantinople, Eastern Orthodox Church)
3	Loren Eiseley born, 1907
4	Richard Wright born, 1908
5	Chief Crazy Horse (Oglala) dies, 1877

LITURGICAL, CULTURAL AND HISTORICAL DATES

6   Hiroshigi remembered (1797–1858); Jane Addams born, 1860

7   United Tribes Days begin; Grandma Moses born, 1860

8   International Literacy Day

9   Chrysanthemum Festival (Japan)

10   Feast Day of Finian of Moville (scholar, early Irish Church)

11   Feast Day of Theodora of Alexandria (Eastern Orthodox Church)

12   Irene Joliot-Curie born, 1897; Jesse Owens born, 1913; The Advocate begins publication, 1967; Steven Biko dies, 1977

13   Dante Alighieri dies, 1321

14   Holy Cross Day (Triumph of the Cross)

15   Claude McKay born, 1889; Anne Moody born, 1940; Birmingham bombing, 1963

16   Hidalgo's Cry for Freedom, 1810; Mexican Independence Day, 1821; B. B. King born, 1925

17   Feast Day of Hildegard of Bingen

18   Congress passes the Fugitive Slave Act, 1850

19   Feast Day of Theodore of Tarsus (Scottish Church)

20   Feast Day of Saints Michael and Theodora (martyrs, Eastern Orthodox Church)

21   International Day of Peace; Feast Day of Matthew the apostle (Church of South India)

22   Autumn equinox (Northern Hemisphere); Ralph Bunche born, 1904; Peace Corps founded, 1961

23   Feast Day of Adamnan, Abbot of Iona (Scottish Church);

	John Coltrane born, 1926
24	Native American Day
25	Little Rock (Arkansas) Central High School integrated by force, 1957
26	Johnny Appleseed born, 1774; T. S. Eliot born, 1888
27	Inauguration of the union of the Church of South India
28	Diarmaid of Feenagh (County Leitrim, Irish Church)
29	Feast Day of Saint Michael and all the angels (Michael, Gabriel and Raphael); Leif Ericson Day
30	Saint Jerome's Day; Elie Wiesel born, 1928 October

October

October is designated as Domestic Violence Awareness Month in the United States. Many Christian churches celebrate the first Sunday in October as Worldwide Communion Sunday and the Sunday before October 31 as Reformation Sunday.

The Jewish holiday of Sukkoth (Feast Day of Tabernacles) is observed on the fifteenth to twenty-second days of Tishri (September to October), to celebrate the end of the agricultural season. Simchat Torah (the beginning of a new year of reading) is observed on the twenty-third day of Tishri. The Hindu festival of lights, Diwali, is celebrated for three nights in October to November to mark the end of the monsoon season.

1	Mohammed's birth; Yosemite National Park founded, 1890; World Habitat Day
2	Mohandas Gandhi born, 1869; Guardian Angels founded
3	Frank Robinson becomes major league baseball's first African American manager, 1974
4	Saint Francis of Assisi dies, 1226; H. Rap Brown born, 1943

5	Feast Day of Saint Charitina (martyr, Eastern Orthodox Church); Tecumseh (Shawnee) dies, 1813
6	Feast Day of Thomas the apostle (Church of South India); William Tyndale dies, 1536; Fannie Lou Hamer born, 1917
7	Desmond Tutu born, 1931; Leroi Jones born, 1934; Toni Morrison wins the Nobel Prize for Literature, 1993
8	Great Chicago fire, 1871; Jesse Jackson born, 1941
9	Feast Day of Denys of Paris (Scottish Church); Leif Erickson Day
10	Canadian Thanksgiving; Eleanor Roosevelt born, 1884; Thelonious Monk born, 1917
11	Feast Day of Saint Philip (Eastern Orthodox Church); Cleve Jones (Names AIDS Memorial Quilt founder) born, 1954
12	Indigenous Peoples Day; Columbus Day; Dick Gregory born, 1932
13	Congan, dies, 735 CE (Scottish Church)
14	W. Penn dies, 1718; first gay and lesbian civil rights march on Washington, D.C., 1979
15	Feast Day of Saint Teresa of Avila (1515–1582); Nelson Mandela and F. W. de Klerk named co-winners of Nobel Peace Prize, 1993
16	World Food Day; Dia de la Raza; Million Man March, 1995
17	Black Poetry Day
18	Feast Day of Saint Luke (Church of South India); Ntozake Shange born, 1948; Wynton Marsalis born, 1961
19	James Meredith escorted into University of Mississippi, 1962

20	Feast Day of Saint Artemius (Eastern Orthodox Church); Christopher Wren remembered (1632–1723)
21	Feast Day of the Black Christ
22	250,000 people boycott in Chicago over school segregation, 1963
23	Swallows leave Capistrano
24	World Disarmament Day; UN Charter signed, 1945
25	Saint Crispin's Day; Northern Ireland repeals its sodomy laws, 1982
26	Feast Day of Kela (female saint, early Irish Church)
27	Feast Day of Nestor, companion of Demetrius (Eastern Orthodox Church); Ruby Dee born, 1927
28	National Immigrants Day; Desiderius Erasmus dies, 1536
29	Feast Day of Taimhthionna (early female saint of Ireland)
30	Racial segregation in the U.S. armed forces ends, 1954
31	All Hallows' Eve; Halloween; Luther nails the ninety-five theses November

November

November is designated as Native American Heritage Month in the United States. Thanksgiving Day is celebrated on the fourth Thursday of November, and the Sunday before Thanksgiving Day is Thanksgiving Sunday.

Advent begins on the fourth Sunday before December 25, the Sunday nearest November 30. The Sunday before the beginning of Advent commemorates the Sovereignty of Christ.

For three nights in October or November, Diwali, the Hindu festival of lights, celebrates the end of the monsoon season.

1	All Saints' Day (lesser saints)

LITURGICAL, CULTURAL AND HISTORICAL DATES 181

2   All Souls' Day (the departed); Day of the Dead (Mexico); Carol Moseley Braun elected to the U.S. Senate, 1992

3   Feast Day of Martin de Porres (patron saint of social justice)

4   Feast Day of Joannicius the Great (Eastern Orthodox Church); Essex Hemphill (poet) dies, 1995

5   World Community Day

6   Derrick Bell (African American professor at Harvard) born, 1930

7   Fionntan of Strasbourg dies, 687 CE (Irish Church)

8   Dorothy Day born, 1897

9   Dorothy Dandridge born, 1923; Kristallnacht (beginning of the Holocaust), 1938

10   Martin Luther born, 1483

11   Veterans Day; Fyodor Dostoevsky born, 1821; Martin Luther King Sr. dies, 1984

12   Feast Day of Machar (c. 600, Scottish Church)

13   Feast Day of John Chrysostom (Eastern Orthodox Church); Whoopi Goldberg born, 1955; Karen Silkwood dies, 1975

14   Booker T. Washington dies, 1915

15   Feast Day of Saint Fergus (Scottish Church)

16   Martyrs of the Jesuit University die (San Salvador), 1989

17   Feast Day of Aengus of Strangford Lough (Irish Church)

18   Hilda dies, 680 (Scottish Church); Howard Thurman born, 1900; Dr. Evelyn Hooker (documented the psychological normality of homosexuality) dies, 1996

19   Feast Day of Abdias (prophet, Eastern Orthodox Church); Sojourner Truth born, 1797; Abraham Lincoln delivers

the Gettysburg Address, 1863

20 Edmund of East Anglia dies, 870 (Scottish Church); Pauli Murray (first African American female priest in the Episcopal Church) born, 1910

21 Feast Day of the Cosmic Christ, Christ the Omega

22 Harry Edwards (sociologist) born, 1942

23 Feast Day of Saint Roinne (Irish Church); U.S. Supreme Court rules in favor of reverse discrimination, 1989

24 Junipero Serra born, 1713; Ron Dellums born, 1935

25 Feast Day of Catherine of Alexandria; John XXIII born, 1881; the ICC bans segregation on all buses, 1955

26 Sojourner Truth dies (American visionary, preacher, abolitionist, 1797–1883)

Dates of Significance for Ethnic/Cultural Groups

These dates are drawn from the preceding calendar to suggest observances that may be especially meaningful for people of various ethnic and cultural identities. These lists are not meant to be exhaustive. Individuals or committees within the congregation may make valuable additions.

African American

January 15	Martin Luther King Jr. born, 1929
February	Black History Month
March 21	Selma-to-Montgomery march begins, 1965
April 3	Martin Luther King Jr.'s "Mountaintop" speech, 1968
May 19	Malcolm X born, 1925

June 19	Juneteenth, 1865
July 9	June Jordan born, 1936
August 11	John Rosamond Johnson born, 1873
September 15	Four girls killed in Birmingham bombing, 1963
October 7	Toni Morrison wins Nobel Prize for Literature, 1993
November 18	Howard Thurman born, 1900
December 1	Rosa Parks sits in the front of the bus and the Montgomery Bus Boycott soon begins, 1955
December 26	Kwanzaa begins (through January 1)

Asian American

January 10–February 19	Chinese New Year
February 19	Japanese American Day of Remembrance (recalling World War II internment camps)
March 20	Patsy Takemoto Mink, first Asian American woman elected to the U.S. House of Representatives, 1964
April	Cherry Blossom Festival
May	Asian-Pacific Heritage Month
June 2	Rice Harvest Festival (Japan)
July 22	Feast Day of Mary Magdalene (South India)
August 6	Hiroshima Day
September 9	Chrysanthemum Festival (Japan)
October 18	Feast Day of Saint Luke (South India)
November	Diwali, Festival of Lights (India)
December 6	Feast Day of Saint Nicholas (Turkey)

Persons with Disabilities

January 4	Louis Braille (teacher, blind) born, 1809
January 8	Stephen Hawking (physicist, ALS) born, 1942
February 11	Thomas Edison born, 1847
June	John Hockenberry (journalist, paraplegic) born, 1956
June 27	Helen Keller (lecturer, blind and deaf) born, 1880
July 19	Mark Wellman (paraplegic) begins climbing El Capitan in Yosemite, 1989
July 26	Americans with Disabilities Act passed, 1990
August 24	Marlee Matlin (actor, deaf) born, 1965
November 13	Whoopi Goldberg (actor, dyslexia) born, 1955
December 10	Thomas Gallaudet (educator of the deaf) born, 1787
December 16	Ludwig van Beethoven (composer, became deaf) born, 1770

European American

January 14	Albert Schweitzer born, 1875
February 21	Peter Damien
March 6	Elizabeth Barrett Browning born, 1806
April 29	Catherine of Sienna dies, 1380
May 16	Joan of Arc born, 1412
June 9	Columba of Iona dies, 597
July 6	Jan Hus born, 1369

August 9	F. Jaegerstetter dies, 1943
September 12	Irene Joliot-Curie born, 1897
October 4	Francis of Assisi dies, 1226
November 8	Dorothy Day born, 1897
December 11	Lars Skrefsrud born, 1910
December 18	Dorothy Sayers born, 1893

Gay/Lesbian

January 3	First lesbian center in the United States (New York City), 1971
February 3	Gertrude Stein born, 1874
February 8	Elizabeth Bishop born, 1911
March 24	ACT UP's first demonstration, 1987
April 30	Countee Cullen born, 1903
May 22	Harvey Milk born, 1930
June	Lesbian and Gay History Month
July 28	Judy Grahn born, 1940
August 6	Minnesota removes transgender discrimination, 1993
September 12	The Advocate begins publication, 1967
October 14	First gay/lesbian civil rights march on Washington, D.C., 1979
November 4	Essex Hemphill (poet) dies, 1995
December 1	World AIDS Day
December 7	Willa Cather born, 1873

Hispanic American

Early January	Las Pastores
March 24	Oscar Romero killed, 1980
March 31	Cesar Chavez born, 1927
April 10	Frida Kahlo (painter) born, 1910
May 5	Cinco de Mayo
June 17	Linda Chavez born, 1947
July 16	Katherine Ortega born, 1934
August 24	Jorge Luis Borges born, 1899
September 15	Hispanic Heritage Month (through October 15)
September 16	Mexican Independence Day, 1821
November 24	Junipero Serra born, 1713
December 12	Feast Day of Our Lady of Guadalupe (Mexico)
December 16	Las Posadas (through December 24)

Jewish American

January 3	Simone Weil born, 1909
Febuary 8	Martin Buber born, 1878
March 2	Scholem Aleichem born, 1859
April 21	Liberation of Bergen-Belsen, 1945
May 3	Golda Meir born, 1898
June 29	Anne Frank born, 1929
July 14	Isaac Bashevis Singer born, 1904
August 25	Leonard Bernstein born, 1925
September 30	Elie Wiesel born, 1928

LITURGICAL, CULTURAL AND HISTORICAL DATES 187

October   Sukkoth (Feast Day of Tabernacles)
November 9   Kristallnacht, 1938
December 21   Henrietta Szold born, 1860

American Indian

Weekly Pow-wows held throughout the year
January 14   Chief Joseph (Nez Perce) dies, 1879
February 17   Geronimo (Apache) dies, 1909
March 30   Spring Corn Dance
April 29   American Indian Movement begins, 1968
May 23   Cherokee Nation forced west, 1839
June 2   Native American citizenship, 1924
July 14   Kateri Tekakwitha (Mohawk) born, 1656
Early August   Intertribal celebrations begin
September 5   Chief Crazy Horse (Oglala) dies, 1877
October 12   Indigenous Peoples Day
November   Native American Heritage Month
December 20   Sacajawea (Shoshoni guide and peacemaker)

Women

January 9   Simone de Beauvoir born, 1908
Febuary 15   Susan B. Anthony born, 1820
March   Women's History Month
March 5   Leontine Kelly (Methodist bishop) born, 1920
April 10   Mechtild of Hackenborn

May 8	Julian of Norwich (1342–after 1416)
June 2	Barbara Harris (Episcopal bishop) born, 1930
July 19	First women's rights conference, 1848
August 26	19th Amendment (women's suffrage), 1920
September 6	Jane Addams born, 1860
October 26	Feast Day of Kela (early female saint, Ireland)
November 2	Carol Moseley Braun, first African American woman elected to the U.S. Senate, 1992
December 2	Four churchwomen killed in El Salvador, 1980

Bibliography

Anderson, David. *Multicultural Ministry: Finding Your Church's Unique Rhythm.* Grand Rapids, Mich.: Zondervan, 2004.

Angrosino, Michael V. *Talking About Cultural Diversity in Your Church: Gifts and Challenges.* Walnut Creek: AltaMira Press, 2001.

Black, Kathy. *Culturally-Conscious Worship.* St. Louis, Mo.: Chalice Press, 2000.

Cenkner, William, ed. *The Multicultural Church: A New Landscape in U.S. Theologies.* New York: Paulist Press, 1996.

Conde-Frazier, Elizabeth, Steve S. Kang, and Gary A. Parrett. *A Many Colored Kingdom: Multicultural Dynamics for Spiritual Formation.* Grand Rapids: Baker Books, 2004.

Cone, James. *God of the Oppressed.* New York: Seabury Press, 1975.

Clay, Ele., ed. *Many Nations Under God: Ministering to Culture Groups in America.* Birmingham, Ala.: New Hope, 1997.

Cyprian, David, and Jamie Phelps, eds. *"Stamped with the Image of God:" African Americans as God's Image in Black.* Maryknoll: Orbis Books, 2003.

Elmer, Duane. *Cross-Cultural Conflict: Building Relationships for Effective Ministry.* Downers Grove: InterVarsity Press, 1993.

Fitzpatrick, Joseph. *One Church, Many Cultures: The Challenge of Diversity.* Kansas City: Sheed and Ward, 1987.

Fritson, Arne, and Samuel Kabue. *Interpreting Disability: A Church of All and for All.* Geneva: World Council of Churches Publications, 2004.

Hawn, Michael C. *One Break, One Body: Exploring Cultural Diversity in Worship.* West Bethesda: The Alban Institute, 2003.

Hirsch, E. D., Jr., Joseph F. Kett, and James Trefil, eds. *Dictionary of Cultural Literacy.* 2d ed. Boston: Houghton Mifflin, 1993.

Hunsberger, George. *Bearing the Witness of the Spirit: Lesslie Newbigin's Theology of Cultural Plurality.* Grand Rapids: Eerdmans, 1998.

Jeung, Russell. *Faithful Generations: Race and New Asian American Churches.* New Brunswick: Rutgers University Press, 2005.

Kim, Jung Ha. *Bridge-Makers and Cross-Bearers: Korean-American Woman and the Church.* Atlanta: Scholars Press, 1997.

King, Martin Luther, Jr. *Where Do We Go From Here: Chaos or Community?* Boston: Beacon Press, 1967.

Law, H. F. Eric. *The Wolf Shall Dwell with the Lamb: A Spirituality for Leadership in a Multicultural Community.* St. Louis: Chalice Press, 1993.

———. *The Word at the Crossing: Living the Good News in a Multicultural Community.* St. Louis: Chalice Press, 2004.

Lee, Jung Young. *Marginality: The Key to Multicultural Theology.* Minneapolis: Fortress Press, 1995.

Matthews, Tony. *There's More Than One Color in the Pew: A Handbook for Multicultural, Multiracial Churches.* Macon: Smyth & Helwys, 2003.

McNeil, Brenda Salter, and Rick Richardson. *The Heart of Racial Justice: How Soul Change Leads to Social Change.* Downers Grove: InterVarsity Press, 2004.

Pope, Liston. *The Kingdom Beyond Caste.* New York: Friendship Press, 1957.

Rhodes, Stephen. *Where Nations Meet: The Church in a Multicultural World.* Downers Grove: InterVarsity Press, 1998.

Rizzuto, Ana-Maria. *The Birth of the Living God.* Chicago: The University of Chicago Press, 1979.

Rusaw, Rick, and Eric Swanson. *The Externally Focused Church.* Loveland, Colo.: Group, 2004.

Satterlee, Craig A. *When God Speaks Through Change: Preaching in Times of Congregational Transition.* Herndon: The Alban Institute, 2005.

Sawyer, Mary R. *The Church on the Margins: Living Christian Community.* Harrisburg: Trinity Press International, 2003.

Spencer, Aida Besancon, and William David Spencer, eds. *The Global God: Multicultural Evangelical Views of God.* Grand Rapids: Baker Books, 1998.

Taylor, E. L. Hebden. *Reformation or Revolution.* Nutley: Craig Press, 1970.

Trible, Phyllis. *God and the Rhetoric of Sexuality.* Philadelphia: Fortress Press, 1978.

Wagner, C. Peter. *Our Kind of People: The Ethical Dimensions of Church Growth in America.* Atlanta: John Knox Press, 1979.

Worley, Robert C. *A Gathering of Strangers: Understanding the Life of Your Church.* Rev. ed. Philadelphia: Westminster Press, 1983.